A SUB

A SUBALTERN ON THE SOMME
IN 1916

By
MARK VII

"Ere we have learnt by use to slight the crimes
And sorrows of the world."—*Wordsworth.*

E · P · DUTTON & COMPANY
NEW YORK

PRINTED AND BOUND IN GREAT BRITAIN BY
ANTONY ROWE LTD, EASTBOURNE

TO
"JOHNNY"
WHO
SANG IN ALL WEATHERS

INTRODUCTORY

*O*DD THE PRANKS THAT MEMORY plays. Odd the features of the past that stand out when we look back over an abyss of years.

Of those now living who assembled at Charing Cross Station soon after nine o'clock on a morning in mid-July 1916, to make the journey that had for its end the Battle of the Somme, are there many to whom the memory of that tremendous occasion prompts the question: "Did we, or did we not, then shave the upper lip?" That one, at any rate, did so speculate may as well be confessed at once; for the reactions to experience this book intends to present must be as candid and truthful as the writer can make them, or authorship on such a subject as the European War will, in his case, be valueless.

The Powers that Were in those days (*facilis descensus!*) have already committed themselves to much educative print, showing us the why and how of high politics and strategy as they affected the fates of some millions of the world's citizens; and we are grateful to them, on the whole, in proportion to their candour. But the lack of candour, in just those places where our curiosity is most piqued, is common to such works, and there is nothing more distressing to the honest listener than to be told, by one who knows more, only the discreet truth. As the lives of great men all re-

mind us, Time has a passion for the indiscreet
truth. It is therefore not surprising that, from the
great men's records of the war, the scraps of candour which fall from their tables are what we
most hungrily devour. Might it also be that a
record of experiences which befell one of the least
in those days would not be without interest if the
writer were capable of telling the simple truth?

That is no small task. Yet even supposing the
possibility of such a chronicler, he should be
warned not to deceive himself. Many of his experiences were doubtless common to millions, and
if it is their attention he would engage, then something other than the bare record of facts will be
required. Facts are mere accessories to the truth,
and we do not invite to our hearth the guest who
can only remind us that on such a day we suffered
calamity. Still less welcome is he who would make
a Roman holiday of our misfortunes. Exaggera-
tion of what was monstrous is quickly recognised
as a sign of egotism, and that contrarious symptom
of the same disease which pretends that what is
accepted as monstrous was really little more than
normal is equally unwelcome. All that is sufferable
in the way of reminiscence must be truth expressed
through personality. And that is art. It gives us
pause.

There comes to our rescue the thought of those
among us, who will soon be men and women, to
whom the war is not even a memory—nothing

but a great adventure just missed through an unlucky accident of birth. They'd like to know, they say; and their children's children rise in vision plying our ears with questions easy to be answered now, but unanswerable when the moss is thick on our graves.

JULY · 1916

A SUBALTERN ON THE SOMME

JULY 1916

Charing Cross

CHARING CROSS STATION: A SOMbre, sunless place, crowded with khaki figures thinly interspersed with civilians, mostly women, dressed in sombre colours. The figures in plain khaki are listless, but those decorated with ribbons, and still more those with red or blue tabs, look animated with the bustle of busy self-importance. To-day the heavy lugubrious atmosphere that often seems to pervade a London terminus is lightning-charged, so that the air vibrates with repressed emotions, felt all the more intensely because no one gives them relief. The hopes and fears of all are the same; but they are not shared: each one bears his own.

Beyond the barrier lie the trains: long black sleeping snakes. We disregard them, as if they were not. They are public servants that have become our masters. We turn away from them because we know that in this scene they are the chief instruments of destiny.

I am hideously self-conscious. One half of me is tunic, belt, puttees, badges, revolver—a figure hoping it presents an approved appearance in the public eye and faintly flattered by the sense of voluntary heroism; the other is a mind seething. This mind has become like a cloud brooding above my body, so full of violence and revolt that constant effort is required to keep it suppressed. Its impulses suggest the maddest actions. Now, as my young wife and I weave an outwardly nonchalant way through the crowd (she does not touch my arm: we know the etiquette), I am on the point of proposing that we walk straight out of the station, get into a taxi and drive and drive and drive till the car breaks down. Even the thought brings a sense of relief, for it opens a vista upon a garden of old enchantment. I draw a shutter across it violently. We go upstairs and drink coffee in the gloomy buffet.

One glance round to see there are no officers of one's own regiment here, then heart's ease for a moment. We can smile to one another. We do not speak. There is nothing to say now. Twenty-two months ago we saw this hour. We were reading *The Globe* after a little dinner at a place near the Marble Arch. We looked up, and as our eyes met we saw this day. That was a lifetime ago; but from that hour every step has been towards this chasm. Then, the rumble of earthquake bringing foreknowledge as clearly as if the red printed page had announced it: now the event, so many times lived in imagination it is difficult to realise it as fact. We look in each other's eyes to reassure one another of reality. The look implies: "You are you. I am I. Nothing else matters."

For all the months of grace between then and now we are not ungrateful. We have reason to give thanks. Love's embodiment now lives. I listened to the flutter of his heart as he lay on my arm last night. Kind was the fate that had kept me from going sooner; for had it been otherwise one victory over death might have been lost. We are free from double dread. For that my heart sings a song often to be sung again in strange places.

We must go. Back through the khaki whirlpool: up the long platform. Ah! There's Brunning the South African, and Zenu the bright, blond beauty, and Leonard the weed, and some more.

Brunning has a full-dress introduction. He is that timely relief, a natural humorist. Besides, he has served in German West Africa, where he lost his right ear. We see in him sound proof that war is not all death. Fat and smiling—Brunning, you're our man for to-day. We'll keep pace with you, though we ride Rosinante.

There is something like a dozen of us in this odd saloon-car with its large, broad windows. We take our places like guests at a conference.

Now the last fierce moment comes. "Step inside, please." Your hand. "Good-bye. Might be back in a fortnight: you never know. Good-bye. Never good-bye." The train moving: a girlish figure running beyond the end of the platform waving, all sadness gone, still waving. . . . Snap! The cord is broken. Back through the window, and here's this collection sitting round like the figures in the poem, "all silent and all . . ." Well, you never know. Some will come back: some won't.

Already I am away in my mind. I know it clearly enough; but the sickly Leonard is sitting beside me starting a whispered confidential burble. It appears he also has an affair of the heart and therefore presumes we must feel alike. He has a grievance, too. It is that younger men than either of us are still at the training-camp. They've no such ties as we have, and Roberts has been fairly crawling round the old colonel to be kept on as adjutant. Roberts is a perfect swine. He has been chortling about the number of fellows he sent out who were killed on the first of July. When he signed Leonard's papers he sniggered over "another death warrant." The whole bloody war was rotten. Of course, it didn't matter to fellows who had no ties. But even if they did get back, who could say what might happen in the meantime with all these crowds of slackers about? The damned Huns! They ought to chuck taking prisoners—that'd soon end it. How long did I think it would last? It couldn't last much longer. Had I been on the musketry course at Catterick? He ought to have gone—ought to be there now— would have been, but for Roberts. It would be good if we got in the same company, wouldn't it? So few fellows understood.'

Feeling much dislike for Leonard and his comparisons, I respond in monosyllables. Yet I am sorry for him, and when at last he stops, I find that his hang-dog misery and petty resentments have been good for nerves stretched, five minutes ago, almost to breaking-point. At least there shall be no grovelling. Well enough I know that I shall never be the real soldier. He lives on pinnacles of indifference I have long decided I shall never reach; but at least one can die decently: at least I've resolution enough for that. Whether I have sufficient to look a man in the face and then blow out his brains with this revolver remains to be seen. What I shall experience at the sight of a bayonet entering my own vitals also remains, possibly, to be known. Now there is no knowing—only possibilities to be faced. Yet a thousand less ghastly things might happen: honours, wounds, hospital, leave, peace. God! Peace itself will come one day. Fancy living to see it! One might.

There is peace outside, there in the fields of Kent. Nature here knows nothing of the war. Through the window I see the fruit-trees dancing in the sunlight. Now they are changed for the rich ranks of hops, bobbing as we pass; and now again the clustering apple-trees. That green and lovely world is at peace; and though the very sunlight seems at times an insult, one would not have

Nature lose her loveliness. The mere knowledge that beauty somewhere still persists is relief.

The Channel

> *Oh ye! who have your eye-balls vex'd and tir'd,*
> *Feast them upon the wideness of the sea.*

It is in its happiest, most bewitching humour. There is just enough movement to show the sea has a life of its own. The sun shines down, master of the dance. I have not seen the sea for nearly two years. This might be a summer holiday, except that astern there's a deadly-looking little destroyer: our escort, I suppose. Mines, torpedoes —the sea is full of man's filth: there is enough to provide a remote possibility we might never reach France. Well, the sea looks bewitching.

A man comes up by my side at the rail. He is a captain in a line regiment, and looks elderly for his rank. His large, mobile features do not suggest the army. He is certainly not of the regular army. for captains in the regular army do not begin conversations with subalterns. He devoutly hopes he is not for the Front this time: he has done his share of fighting in Gallipoli. He believes there's a good chance of his being appointed Director of Entertainment Parties for troops just out of the line: close up, of course, but not actually under fire.

I wonder at his frankness. Somebody's got to do the fighting. Is everyone in France quite as ready to leave it to somebody else? He explains that he is over forty, and after Gallipoli rather thought they might give him a job at home. He is an actor and went to enlist straight from a London theatre on the day war broke out. Oh yes! Of course; now I remember him. I am pleased and flattered by his geniality, for in the theatre he is a person of importance. Who'd have thought, that day when I sat in the pit, I should next see him here? He talks to me now, I suppose, because most men become sociable in time of misfortune.

Boulogne

What a change has come over Boulogne since August 1st, 1914! It has been converted from a guest-house into a workshop. As we steamed up the harbour on the day of France's mobilisation nearly two years ago, cheers greeted us from the pier, blue figures on the quay waved their flags and a band played. Boulogne was French, and full of French excitement and cordiality. To-day, as we silently drifted in like cargo, and like cargo lay waiting I know not what formalities before we could land, I felt that Boulogne had been Anglicised. Now, after lunching at the British Officers' Club, as I drift about the town waiting for the train that is to take us to Étaples, it seems as if the French element had retired to its fastness before an invader. The place wears a big British mask, and the mask shows the broad commercial features of John Bull. Boulogne is busier than it has ever been; but it has lost its character in the exigencies of war.

That the war is not very far away I am made conscious as I enter the station. An ambulance-train has just come in and suddenly "walking cases" appear, their heads or arms swathed in bandages. They look like men let out of prison, so much bustle and vigour they have: so much anxiety to get along. The blood still stains their dressings and shocks by its gross reality. The hours of idling in Boulogne made an anti-climax in our journey: we seemed to have missed our way to the Front. Now these blood-stained heads come as a sharp reminder of our destination. Quite surely we are bound for the places these men have left.

Étaples

Dusk is falling as we detrain at Étaples. We have been a long time making the short journey, and are glad to shake our limbs after being wedged tight in those uncomfortable wooden carriages. We drop out by the side of the rails and scuttle up a sandy slope, where we report and receive details of our quarters for the night. We wander through a sea of canvas, our valises following, and now by the light of a candle unroll them on the wooden floor of a bell-tent. Zenu, Hill and two others share this tent with me. They are soon asleep. Even the longest day comes to an end at

last. A gramophone at a Y.M.C.A. hut some way
down on the side of this sandy hill is playing tunes
from *The Maid of the Mountains*. It stops.
Through the door-flap of the tent I can see the
stars. Hill snores loudly as I get into my bag.
What a release to feel alone and free from military busyness! Passionately I try to send waves of
something deeper than thought across the estrang-
ing miles, and in the effort fall asleep.

"The Bull Ring"

It is nine o'clock on a day that promises heat.
We are on our way to the Bull Ring: two hundred
of us, officers who have not been to the Front and
are therefore due for a course of intensive training till some battalion of our regiments shall re-
quire us. Here we are, slogging along under the
command of a captain, back in the ranks again,
carrying rifles. This appears to be an indignity to
some of these fellows; but it does not trouble me,
for I have no gift for the assertion of authority,
and find it easier to obey army orders than to
give them. The responsibility of command is an
effort which diverts thought from what are much
more natural, if useless, channels.

These huts to our right and left are hospitals.
And what is that, looking like an ungrown hop-
field? A British cemetery, Lord! How many have
died already! The ground is smothered with
wooden crosses. We march on in the heat till we

come to a great open sandy arena. Out on to this
plain we file, and now we are put through physical
jerks by officers who have risen from the regular
ranks; and now are drilled by sergeant-majors
who have been chosen for this duty presumably
by virtue of the harshness of their voices and the
austerity of their manners. It is hot work, and
there is a fierce, vindictive atmosphere about this
place which makes its name of " Bull Ring " intel-
ligible. Later we climb up among the sand dunes
on the other side of the road, and there practise
firing rifle grenades and throwing those small egg-
shaped cast-iron missiles known as Mills' bombs.
Here too we learn more of the methods of gas
attack and defence, and practise the art of shoving
our heads quickly into the clammy flannel bags
that are dignified by the name of P. H. helmets.
We finish the morning's work by running obstacle
races over a prepared course back on the arena.

In other times, all signs of our activity banished,
these sand dunes must make a place of delightful
holiday. Even to-day one's eyes wandered instinctively toward the blue estuary that lay below
us, where the tiny white sail of a yacht moved
slowly up-stream.

Gramophones

The tents in this camp are uncountable. All
the way down this sandy slope, up the next hillock

and down over the other side, beyond, away and on all sides they stretch, interspersed here and there with more solid buildings: canteens, army ordnance depots and Y.M.C.A. huts. It is a city of canvas whose inhabitants are always changing. Men and officers, they are here to-day and gone to-morrow. We are all waiting. A batch of Somersets arrived last night. To-day they belong to the Black Watch and have gone up the line in kilts. The casualties since July 1st have been too heavy to allow every draft to go to its own regiment.

Off parade there is little to do. We write letters: eat and drink in the mess: talk or play cards in the hut. And whether we like it or not, we listen to the eternal gramophone. At every hour of the day, and half the night, some gramophone is going. Up the slope the pitiful wail is carried on the breeze:

If you were the only girl in the world
And I were the only boy.

A pathetic hymn before battle. Yet it serves as a reminder that, under many layers of treacly sentiment, the human heart still beats: even this war cannot remove that organ. Nero did well to play the fiddle: the gramophone is our best substitute. And that pathetic tune, who knows but its terrible popularity is due to the subconscious craving in every one of us here for his own suspended individual life?

Paris-Plage

We might be in England. Someone has had the good taste to open a tea-shop in Paris-Plage that, but for its military customers, puts the thought of camps and army routine a thousand miles away. The cretonnes about the windows are in strong simple colours, and the china might have come from a Cottage Tea Room. Half a dozen of us have walked and trammed to Paris-Plage solely for the luxury of feeling English civil ease again. What creatures of environment we are! We could buy the same food in the mess for half the money; yet no one would mistake us for dilettanti.

There is little attraction about Paris-Plage itself. The front is deserted: the normal life of the place is suffering war repression. Like every English seaside town during the war, Paris-Plage wears by daylight the fancy dress of last night's dance. We wander round and the time hangs heavy on our hands. Nothing is more desolate than forsaken gaiety. Let's jump on the little tram and go back to camp.

On the road to Balancourt

We are on the road from Longprès to Balancourt, Zenu, Hill and myself, marching at the rear of a motley detachment made up of men belonging to three regiments. They are being drafted into the battalion of the line regiment

we also are joining to-day. Leonard and Brunning
have already been posted to this battalion, which
was badly cut up on July 1st, and is now out
on rest, being re-formed.

Conversing at the first halt, we discover that
these men have come from all directions. Some
are little more than boys and have yet to see
fighting: some have come *via* hospital from Gallipoli; others from Egypt; and they vary in ages
from seventeen to forty-five. It is a close afternoon: they seem to be badly out of training, and
those from Egypt suffer with soft feet. We have
not done more than half the six miles when one
of the boys faints. He lies in the dust, his face
red and puffy, while I undo his tunic, wondering
why he should have collapsed. The reason is soon
obvious. He is wearing one of those much-adver-
tised body-shields, a thing that in the trenches
might stop a very tired bullet, though here its
only purpose has been to impede the lad's breathing and overheat his body. I wonder what pathetic
history attaches to this unhappy life-preserver.
Some anxious woman has obtained a promise from
the boy to wear it. Alas, the thrusts of death in
this encounter are not quite so easily parried as
the merchants of this pitiful armour would have
you, good mother, to believe.

Joining the Regiment

I had formed a mental picture of how a subaltern joined his regiment. First he met the adjutant, who took careful particulars of training
and special qualifications. Then, with due cere-
mony, he was taken into another room and formally introduced to the colonel, who deigned to
extend his hand and wish the young man luck.
Then the colonel would follow this with some
details of the battalion's immediate history, a foot-
note on esprit de corps and the honour of the regiment, and finally give a few words of fatherly
advice. The subaltern saluted and returned to the
adjutant, who now gave the junior particulars of
his company, told him how he could obtain an
orderly, what were the regimental messing arrangements and any other local details.

But it does not happen like that.

As the draft reaches the top of the last hill, we
are met by a sallow-faced cadaverous-looking
young man on a horse, who in a Cockney accent
shouts directions to the troops. He tells Hill and
me we are for C Company and will report to
Captain Rowley. We inquire the way of men on
the road and are directed to a farmhouse standing
beyond the midden that fills the courtyard of a
French farm. We pick our way across the dung-
heap and enter a room that seems to be fulfilling
nearly all the purposes of human habitation at
once. There are two large wooden bedsteads and

two camp-beds, unmade; dirty water in a tin washing-basin, unemptied chamber-pots, unwashed linen, food, whisky-bottles, glasses, papers, bedding, equipment strewn all over the place. Captain Rowley lies fully dressed on the sheets of one of the unmade beds, dozing. We tell him who we are and he replies in a mild friendly voice, but hardly takes a look at us; he is evidently very tired.

Another subaltern comes in. He is a bright, fresh-faced youth, fair-haired and slim, with the down still on his upper lip. He tells us he has been with the battalion a week or two, having seen service in the trenches last year with one of the London territorial regiments. He has a public-school accent and a sly, half-humorous expression. His name is Hardy.

A moment later another subaltern, Mallow, the bombing-officer, comes in. He begins to hold a conversation with Rowley which is one of the frankest I have ever heard. It appears that on the previous evening they rode into a neighbouring town where they spent the night with women of easy affections, and now they proceed to recount the details of their adventures and discuss the possibilities of similar entertainment, with a coarseness which is without reserve. They drink big tots of whisky, but seem too dissipated to raise more than a mirthless laugh. Hardy tries to join in, but meets with only tolerant patronage.

The whole scene strikes me as a study for Teniers.

Two of a kind

Hill and I stroll out of the village: our dignity is offended. We are neither of us prudes, but the obscenity was too rank. Moreover, Hill too had cherished some idea of being decently installed in the regiment, and is very sore about our reception.

We come to a bank overlooking a cornfield and sit down. The lush green of the earth, the colour in the evening sky and the songs of birds in the thicket behind us make the peace of twilight like a presence felt. It begets confidences, and the shy Hill hints at a love-affair and gives me an address he would like me to write to if anything should happen to him. He tells me of his home and his life as a shipping-clerk in the City. It is all very ordinary; but just now the knowledge that another human being here has lived an ordered human life with its natural affections is welcome by its contrast. I realise that we are just a pair of homesick children.

The Sergeant-Major

On the first parade of our company one figure stands out. It is Company-Sergeant-Major Steel. He is a tall, thin, dark man of about five-and-twenty, with a long hooked nose and a slight stoop. He wears the D.C.M., but his manner is casual, and there is nothing of the parade ser-geant-major about him: indeed, I wonder at first how a man of such weedy appearance can have at-tained his rank. But when Rowley introduces us, I see a couple of keen, intelligent eyes looking abnormally bright, like eyes that have seen too much. As we step aside, Rowley describes him to me as the bravest man in the regiment, who ob-tained his distinction by bringing in fourteen prisoners, single-handed, on July 1st.

In days to come I am to see much of this man. Many a dreary hour in the trenches we shall wile away together, talking of his home in the West of England where he used to be a confectioner, and where his young wife and child wait for him. There's strange galvanism in this man, for he can pull the whole company together with a word, and yet his natural habit of mind is soft and re-flective. Already he is utterly sick of the war and many a time he is to tell me, in response to some chaff about his ribbon, how gladly he would ex-change it for a week's leave.

The C.O.

It is the second day after our arrival. Word comes round while we are at breakfast, "All officers to the C.O. at 8.30." Now I shall see the colonel. At present I don't know who he is. Officers, many of whom I have not seen before, crowd into a small room, each one saluting as he comes before a grey-headed, red-faced man, wearing a Scottish uniform, who sits writing at a table. Standing by his side is another Scotsman, tall, raw-boned and of very sour expression. He is our medical officer. The faces of the two men offer a contrast in red and grey; but they both look unpleasant.

Without preamble the colonel begins:

" The discipline in this battalion is damnable. Some of you officers don't **know** your job at all. You think the men will respect you just because you wear a belt. They won't, and I don't blame them. You've got to command these men before they'll respect you, and the sooner you make up your minds to it the better. I see officers talking to men as their equals. I won't have that. If there isn't an alteration at once I intend to make it devilish hot for you. I don't know what you've learnt at home. I don't know who sent you out here. Some of you fellows have only just come out. Well, you may as well understand, this isn't a picnic. If you don't know your job and show a very different idea of discipline, I'll have you sent back and reduced to the ranks. You think you've come to France to loaf about. You'll find your mistake. There's got to be a drastic alteration, or back you go. I'll not allow the men to be under the command of inefficient officers. Just understand that.—You can go."

We salute and file out. This seems a strange

introduction. What does he know about our efficiency? The majority of us have only been with the battalion a matter of days. Why should we be cursed by a man who has never set eyes on us? We are volunteers; most of us joined in '14, and our prospects of dying for our grateful country are the brightest in the world. Is this the way the modern commander spurs his men on to victory? As a matter of fact, Hill and Zenu, I happen to know, are particularly good responsible officers, and Brunning is no chicken.

I am stung with resentment. Rowley sees this and smiles indulgently. He declares it is all "eyewash," prompted by the doctor who regards every man who was not in France before July as a skunk. But the knowledge of what I have given up to come out here is too strong for my sense of humour, and my anger, at what seems to me studied insult, seethes.

Captain Rowley

I am getting to know my captain. He is just a good-natured fellow, with any amount of pluck, whose morals have been damaged by the war and its whisky. The amount of whisky he and Mallow, the bombing-officer, can drink is astonishing. Every time Mallow reaches for the bottle he repeats the parrot phrase, "This war will be won on whisky or it won't be won at all," apparently intending to float home on whisky himself. Mallow is a pretty coarse-fibred creature; but Rowley is of different material. There's been tragedy in this fellow's life and it has knocked off his rudder. His hair is prematurely grey; his complexion ashy; and although there is still a twinkle in his eye, it is fading, and in repose his face wears the expression of an injured animal. Crossed, he shows a streak of cruelty, but at heart he is full of kindliness. He carries out his duties as a company commander with a queer mixture of punctiliousness and slackness. I wish his conversation was not quite so filthy, for temperamentally I believe we are friends.

Moving up

We are marching out of Balancourt, and for the first time I am at the head of my own platoon, number eleven. Hardy has number nine, Hill ten, and twelve is at present in charge of a sergeant. It is the glorious afternoon of a perfect July day. The sky is flecked with white clouds whose shadows chase across the undulating wooded country. The tall corn is ripening, and between its stalks poppies and cornflowers glow with colour. Through the valley we are descending a noisy stream finds its way, and on the hills beyond, great elm-trees stand like wise men brooding. It is a lush green country, full of beauty. The war seems far away.

How this natural beauty soothes the mind! Where beauty is, life and death are not estranged; they seem, as now, treble and bass of the same harmony. War breaks that harmony; but only for a time, and who could not endure the pause with scenes like this deep-dyed upon his memory?

"Left, right! Left, right! Keep closed up! By your right!" I shall gain the confidence, and more —the affection of these men. What do I care if they now think me green? What does it matter if they are a mixed lot, mostly undersized? We are all men. We shall see it through together. If I can mitigate the hardness of their lot, that's my job. I loathe their beastly packs and rifles as much as they do. Cheerio! my hearties. We'll see it through together. And I fall to wondering what number eleven and its officer looked like a month ago.

South Africans

We are approaching Condé when a small company of Scottish troops appear, coming along the road towards us. We halt together, and they prove to be the pioneers of the South African Scottish. Their major comes over to Rowley to inquire where we are bound for. We show him our newly issued trench-maps of the country round Martinpuich, and his comment is that we've got a long way to go. His battalion has had a terrible time in Delville Wood. More than half are casualties, and he doesn't yet know which of his brother officers are dead or alive.

Condé

I hear Rowley shouting from the next room that it is time to get up. We are sleeping on the red-tiled floor of a farmhouse at Condé and it is still pitch dark. We draw ourselves out of our valise-bags and dress in the shadows of candle-light. It is still dark as I go down the street to see my platoon which has slept in a barn. Dark figures move about with lanterns as we form up in line ready to move off. "Form fours! Right! By the right, quick march!" Here and there heads are poked out of windows as we tramp out of the town.

The dawn breaks pale and misty. We are halted beside a railway embankment, waiting to entrain at Hangest for some station near the battle-line. Rowley smiles grimly as we discuss our prospects over a cold breakfast. He has seen Hooge and Ypres. "All you poor beggars (only he never said "beggars") will be dead in a week," he says cheerily. "Three hours' bombardment and you'll break the bones of your legs with your knees knocking together. You're in for a bloody fine time, I can tell you. Cheerio! Let's have that whisky. *You'll* want whisky when you get into those trenches. And by the way—no prisoners.

If any of you come back with prisoners to me, you'll be in for it. We're not taking any more prisoners in this regiment, and the Hun knows it. Shoot the beggars. If you bring 'em to me, *I*'ll shoot 'em—and you, too."

I remember the jibe of a London cabman, "Brave words off a weak stomach," and laugh, saying I shall certainly bring in any prisoners that come my way. There is a waver in his eyes which puts me quite at ease, though he, not certain whether he is serious or not, repeats the threat.

Prisoners' cages

While we are forming up outside Méricourt station I see for the first time a prisoners' "cage." Surely this is the foulest insult to mankind the war has begotten. The cage is like a poultry-run, only laced in disordered strands with wire that is "barbed" after the pattern of the crown of thorns.

A sentry stands at the gate with fixed bayonet, and his smart and soldierly appearance stands out in terrible contrast with that of the creatures who loll about or sit on the bare ground within, hatless, ragged and lousy.

A viler invention than barbed wire was never conceived: it is the perfect symbol of cruelty. The man who first devised it must have received a peerage in hell. And here it is used to provide a place of rest and habitation for the lords of creation. These "lords" have sunk below the status given to the monkeys at the Zoo; and certainly, in their decrepitude and dejection, the inmates of this cage cannot compare with the nimble beasts whose cages have no barbs. I cannot get by without a shudder. This is the bottom of degradation. Call them Huns if you like: there remains a limit to the indignity judges may impose upon criminals without grave moral damage to the judges. These cages pass that limit. We should show more natural feeling if we lined these poor devils up in a row and shot them. That at least would acknowledge their manhood.

I should like to be allowed to go inside and apologise, explaining that the beastly necessities of the times have driven us to means we abhor.

Dernancourt

We are bivouacking on the side of a chalk hill about a mile west of Dernancourt. The wide valley of the Ancre stretches out before us, the sluggish river itself running where those pollard willows stand, two hundred yards from the road that passes at the foot of this hill. Albert lies hidden about a couple of miles north-east, and the battle-line is now somewhere beyond those hills on our left.

The boom of the guns is continuous. We are not far from our destination, for we can see the absurd sausage-balloons that are let up on their cords into the sky and slowly drawn to earth again when observation is over. Aeroplanes, too, are busy, usually flying singly; the red, white and blue rings of the Allied planes just distinguishable in the sky. Occasionally two or three German machines will penetrate our line as far as this, and then there is a clatter of anti-aircraft guns and puffs of white smoke form little clouds around the hawk-like objects in the blue that have the white Maltese crosses on their breasts. The "archies" make it too hot for them to come far, though we never see a hit.

The road below is a highway to the battle. Day and night a continuous stream of traffic trundles by; guns, limbers, wagons, lorries, they flow along. Destruction has a big appetite and feeds incessantly.

On the hillside, kits are set out in rows just as the men were halted, and there they sleep in the open, for the weather is gloriously fine. We officers of C Company prefer the open to a tent and have planted ourselves under a bank near the crest of the hill. Now it is afternoon and the men have gathered in circles to play a game, new to me, known as "House." It seems to be a strange game, for it is accompanied by a lot of shouting on the part of one who presumably acts in the capacity of "bookie," counting and shouting all the time.

Other men sit on their ground-sheets addressing

those highly coloured silk-sewn cards that will one day adorn many an English cottage mantel-shelf. These cards, with their bright hues, sentimental messages and French character, are very popular: they supply a compendious want. They also save platoon-officers from the business of censoring, which tends to become irksome whenever the men have much time on their hands. Censoring letters is an unpleasant, impertinent duty, to be hurried over and treated as formally as possible. By constant repetition it becomes a deadly bore. Occasionally there is a patch of rich unconscious humour, but the formula is almost unvaried. The writer is in the pink, in spite of everything: a condition he hopes is mutual. He believes there's a war on, so we must keep smiling. Hopes and fears for leave are always expressed, and promises of battle-souvenirs are usually remembered. There is the inevitable P.S.: "The cakes were all right, but a bit smashed, and I'd like some Woodbines: the fags they serve out here are rotten."

Ugly punishments

There is a boy from D Company doing Field Punishment No. 1 down by the road this afternoon. His outstretched arms are tied to the wheel of a travelling field-kitchen. The regimental-sergeant-major has just told me that the boy is there for falling out on the march. He defended himself before the C.O. by saying that he had splinters of glass in his feet; but the M.O. decided against him. Quite possibly the boy is a liar; but wouldn't the army do well to avoid punishments which remind men of the Crucifixion?

And these two men being marched up and down in the blazing heat, under the raucous voice of the provost-sergeant, they disturb all peace of mind. I do not know from what offences they are doing "pack-drill," but it is depressing to see them, loaded with rifles and full packs, going to and fro over a piece of ground not more than twenty yards long, moving like automata under that awful voice.

Volunteers going shortly into battle! It is not a pleasant picture. It calls to mind too vividly those propagandist posters of the "bonny boys." Besides, surely this war wants all our energy. The most fearfully arduous task, if it served some purpose, would be preferable to these senseless evolutions, designed merely to fatigue. Volunteers going into battle! I think with almost physical sickness of the legends that sustain our arm-chair patriots at home.

AUGUST

AUGUST

Castlereagh and others

I AM GETTING TO KNOW THE MEN of my platoon. About a third of them, the pick of the bunch, are miners from the north of England: short, tough, reserved men, used to hard work and not given to "grousing." More than half of them are married. Collins, with the mild voice of a curate, is a widower, and by religion a Methodist. Burt stands next him on parade. He is the platoon Hercules: a hard drinker with the neck of a bull. He wants me to issue a boxing challenge on his behalf to anyone in the regiment. Spencer is a tall, red-faced lad, awkward but intelligent. I presume the pits have given him that incurable stoop. These are among the miners.

The trades of the rest make an extraordinary list. Labourer, wheelwright, railway storekeeper, farmer, platelayer, cabinet-maker, rag-conditioner, oil-presser, painter, shoe-salesman, driller, grinder, wool-sorter—what occupations a civil world provides! Then Barlow calls himself a "horseman," and, being the platoon fool, can give no more explicit description of himself. Anyway, it is unlikely that he will be wanted for the cavalry: and I should be sorry if he were, for he is an unconscious comedian. Jenkins again is an "interpreter"—of languages, perhaps; but I rather suspect the description as being designed for purposes of reference when those "chits" from the orderly room come round, promising comfortable billets for men of strange trades. I suspect this because Jenkins shows himself a cute student of his own well-being in other ways.

That little wisp of a man, Jackson, who has been to India with the regular army, is something of an enigma. He is smart enough, but he wears a bored expression and seems strangely reticent and unresponsive. To-day, when I told him I wanted him to take a stripe, seeing that in point of service he was nearly the oldest soldier in the platoon, he replied that he would rather not. Well, he must, for there's nobody else.

Corporal Neal, who escaped injury on July 1st with the old battalion, has lost his nerve, if he ever had it. He is demonstrative in his authority; but I do not like his stupid, shifty eyes or his subservient manner. Still less do I like the sergeant I am saddled with by the colonel. He has a criminal look, and why he should suddenly be promoted from the ranks to full sergeant I cannot imagine. He has served in Gallipoli, but we do not know his record. Like Neal, he is too servile, and I am a bad judge of men if he proves trustworthy.

Another from the batch that joined the regiment with me I have taken for my orderly. Herbert Castlereagh (better known to his mates as "Erb") is a dark undersized Cockney with a switch of black hair that the company barber ought to see to. His personal cleanliness is an item he forgets, and his speech is difficult to understand; but he has a comical face and there is a good deal of the faithful spaniel about him. He says he is twenty-one: he doesn't look more than sixteen. With a true Cockney's ability to make shift, he found some sticks and rigged me up quite a tolerable bath this morning; and though the performance entailed mild censure for indecent exposure, I'm pleased with Castlereagh, and we shall repeat the trick. An orderly has a few privileges, and, after Gallipoli, it seems only human to save such a brat from as much hardship as possible. He is the butt of the other orderlies, but in his old serio-comic fashion he is quite able to defend himself. He has a marvellous stock of righteous indignation that he displays like a coster if I, or another, happen to swear at him. A queer self-contained bit of old humanity, I like him, and believe he likes me.

Nearing the beginning

We have been on this hillside ten days, getting in all the training possible, adding to our strength, shaping up the companies and, not the least pleasantly, bathing in the river below. Hardy has been made acting-adjutant. The new colonel has arrived, and we are determined to like him because he is a regular officer of this regiment. I am afraid it will be hard work, for he has fishy eyes and a weak chin; still, everybody is glad the old Scotchman has gone. Other new officers have arrived, among them Smalley, who has taken over number twelve platoon of this company. He is an Englishman who came back from Australia at the outbreak of the war and has seen service in the ranks of the Guards: an excellent fellow who knows his job and is without frills or outstanding vices. The battalion is still considerably below strength, but I hear we are moving forward tomorrow.

What a strange emotion all objects stir when we look upon them wondering whether we do so for the last time in this life! I catch myself having a fierce desire to rivet impressions, even of commonplace things like the curve of a roof, the turn of a road, or a mere milestone.

> *But at my back I always hear*
> *Time's wingèd chariot hurrying near;*
> *And yonder all before us lie*
> *Deserts of vast eternity.*

The panorama

The sun is setting over Albert.

I have wandered out alone to the top of this hill, learning that a view of the battle-front may be had from this spot. Nearly all the rough ground hereabouts is taken over by some department of the army; dumps and camps are littered about everywhere like a child's toys strewn over the nursery floor. But here, for a few hundred yards, where the scrub is clear, poppies and cornflowers stud the ground about my feet and glow bright as jewels in the evening light. Behind the ruined spire of the cathedral, torn as if some beast had mauled its flanks, the sun goes down in a blaze. Banners of the richest and palest hues float out and flutter there in long and narrow waves that ebb in the receding light. From palest green to deep blood-red they blend their harmonies. They ravish the eye and melt the heart.

I turn from them to look out over the east.

The sky is purple dark and all along the horizon gun-flashes quiver as if some fearful aurora borealis were continually appearing. Every now and then huge explosions send up pillars of smoke, as though the internal fires of the earth had broken through. Nearer, the darkness is pricked by lesser lights that rise to fall and fade successively, like matches thrown into the air; and to all these ominous illuminations there comes the continual accompaniment of roll and roar: the grind and belch of guns and the shock of countless explosions.

It is an inferno. Can anything live in that? Heaven on one side: hell on the other. One should not hope to come out of that alive. It is a continuous earthquake.

Well, life must end somewhere. One wouldn't have chosen it there. But how to be rid of this ceaseless resentment against being pulled back by death just as one had one foot on the threshold of life? How to die whole?

That wholeness seems best found in praising what has been. Yes, life has been good; rich, sweet and good. Seen now through memory's prism it glows with colours rich as the sunset's. And with that to fortify the will there must be no bitterness, no unassuageable regret.

There is peace—even joy if we can only release our hold with childlike gentleness.

Near Albert

We have moved another step forward. This field by the cross-roads, where we sleep in the open, is called Belle Vue Farm, though I see no farm. As to the *belle vue*, that has been spoilt. The town of Albert, which lies below us to the north, has been raked with shell-fire and looks half ruins. Some chimney-stacks still stand. They sway beneath the gilded figure of the Mother and Child. That figure once stood triumphant on the cathe-

dral tower; now it is bowed as by the last extremity of grief. Troops still occupy the cellars
of the town, but shells drop into the place every
day. I woke just now to an eerie watery sound, followed by a long whizzing rush, and then a thud:
shells falling behind us. I did not recognise them
at once, their watery gurgle through the air as
they passed overhead seemed so slow and tame.

The old front line

Hardy and I are off to Pommiers Redoubt,
Mametz, where we are to report that the battalion
will arrive this evening. We descend the long hill
leading to Fricourt, dodging about the stream of
traffic that stirs the dust of the road to a thick
haze. Near the bottom of the hill we come upon
the old front line of July 1st. The country here
is stricken waste: the trees that formed an avenue
to the road are now torn and broken stumps, some
still holding unexploded shells in their shattered
trunks, others looped about with useless telegraph-
wire. The earth on both sides of the road is
churned up into a crumbling mass, and so tossed
and scarred is the ground that the actual line of
the front trenches is hardly distinguishable. On
the far side, in the face of a steep rise, we see the
remains of what were deep German dug-outs; but
everything needs pointing out, for the general
impression is of a wilderness without verdure or
growth of any kind. To our right we notice a

ruined cemetery. It looks as if it might have heard
the Last Trump. Graves are opened and monuments of stone and beaded wire lie smashed and
piled in heaps.

Now, as we near Mametz, we come upon guns
hidden under the banks of the roadside and
camouflaged above by netting. The road through
Mametz is still under enemy observation; so we
turn sharply to the right to go round the back of
the rising ground that faces us. All that remains
of the village of Fricourt is a pile of bricks; there
appear to be just about enough to build one house;
and Mametz Wood is nothing more than a small
collection of thin tree-trunks standing as if a forest
fire had just swept over them. On the right of the
sunken road we have now taken is a mound of
sinking freshly-turned earth. It marks the grave
of the Devons who died in the capture of Montauban. A little farther on we come upon all that
remains of a German field cemetery: two or three
painted triangular wooden crosses; the other
graves will now go unmarked for ever. Here we
leave the road and begin to climb over the forsaken trenches. Barbed wire, bombs, bully-beef
tins, broken rifles, rounds of ammunition, unexploded shells, mess-tins, bits of leather and web-
bing equipment, British and German battered steel
helmets, iron stakes, and all the refuse of a battlefield, still litter the mazy ground. I come across

a skull, white and clean as if it had lain in the desert.

We can only move slowly over this confusion of forsaken trenches running in every direction, but at last we are clear of them and mount the hill which is our objective. It broadens out to a wide plateau. Little holes are cut in the ground just big enough to shelter one or two men and presumably give them cover from observation. The large old German dug-outs are not at first visible. We report at one of them and return along the hot road by the way we came.

Trenches on the Somme

We are going to the trenches. That little knot of men two hundred yards ahead, just disappearing over the barren crest of the rise, is Hill's platoon. Two hundred yards behind us is Smalley's. This afternoon the sun glares down on earth that has lost its nature, for, pitted everywhere with shell-holes, it crumbles and cracks as though it has indeed been subject to earthquake. Up here we can be seen by the enemy; but there is no hurrying, for we have to keep distance between platoons. Hill has halted: we must halt, too. The men behind me swear with nervous irritation and mutter about being stuck out here to be fired at, I turn to look at them. Standing loaded up with boxes

of bombs and sandbags of rations, how utterly
unlike the red-coats of romance they appear.

We are off again, now traversing the slope that
leads to the valley of Longueval. "Death Valley,"
it is nicknamed, and it has earned its title, for
everywhere there are signs of death: an inverted
bottle with a bit of paper in it: a forage-cap hung
on a stick: a rough wooden cross bearing the pen-
cilled inscription, "To an Unknown British Soldier." These signs recur: pathetic, temporary
memorials; will they outlast the war? In the bottom of the valley lie broken trucks and the shattered rails of a tramway. As we come to the end
of the tram-line we have to pass the body of a
dead horse, foul and distended, poisoning the air.
Suddenly, like a rat, a human figure comes out of
the earth. Who would have thought there were
dug-outs here? As quickly it disappears and we
pass on. We march in silence, broken occasionally
by a jest that fails to catch on, or by an irritable
rebuke from one jogged by his companion. There
is no singing now; 'tis as if we moved under an
invisible cloud.

We halt for a moment in a chalk-pit where the
M.O. has his dug-out, and then follow the narrow-
ing sunken road that leads up St. George's Hill.
By the time we have reached the top we are moving in single file round the horseshoe bend of the
trench we are to occupy, pushing by the troops
that wait for us to relieve them.

This is an old German trench that has been reversed and now forms part of our second line facing High Wood, just distinguishable as such, about five hundred yards away on the hill opposite. We have hardly entered the trench before we come on a stretcher lying on the ground. It bears the body of a boy: the face quite black. He has just been killed. It appears there was an old German latrine close to the parapet of the trench; two boys had gone to it when a shell came over and killed them both. As we push along I find that this particular sector falls to my platoon. The shell has made a big breach. To-night we shall have to repair it and clean up the mess which is beyond description.

The men are posted and the relieved troops scuttle out. In this narrow gap between two deep walls of clay we shall spend the next four days. The air is tainted with the sickly-sweet odour of decaying bodies. At certain corners this odour intensified by the heat, becomes a stench so foul the bay cannot be occupied. Just now I tripped over a lump in the floor of the trench. It was necessary to get a shovel and quickly cover the spot. Literally we are the living among the dead.

Shelling is incessant. There is not a moment when something is not passing overhead; but the fire is not upon this trench, it is meant for the batteries now crammed up close behind on the rearward slope of the hill. Our batteries are replying, shell for shell. Somewhere very close to my sector a French seventy-five barks deafeningly.

I look for a place to lay my ground-sheet and rations, and find a hole burrowed in the side of the parapet and a new German saxe-blue coat lying on the floor. This hole will give cover from shrapnel and serve to deaden the noise if there's any chance of sleep; but it would prove an ugly death-trap if a shell dropped near. I lay my things in the hole and turn to see Rowley and the company-sergeant-major coming along to inspect. We go round together till we come to a spot in a traverse behind my sector where the smell of decay is so strong they are convinced there is a body lying out. Sure enough, just behind the parados, the dead body of a gunner lies on a stretcher evidently left in haste. Both shin-bones are broken, but otherwise the poor fellow looks unhurt. We have the corpse carried out along the narrow trench: a difficult, awkward business.

I see Jackson considering the gap in our parapet and speak to him about it. He has the whole thing sized up, and without any fuss makes himself responsible for a particularly filthy job, telling me just what he proposes to do as soon as it is dark. He seems more at his ease in the trenches. I shall like this man.

Wondering how Hill fares I go down the trench to see him, and we decide we shall have to spread out our platoons, that are much under strength if we are to keep in touch. I am just returning along the unoccupied gap between us when rapid rifle-fire suddenly starts in the valley below. What does it mean? I get up on a firestep and peer over. There's nothing to see, but the firing continues, causing a cloud of smoke that begins to fill the air. Are they coming over? If they do—well, I've this bit of the line to myself. I pull out my revolver, load it and wait, wondering ironically what anyone would give for my chances. If they come as soon as this, it will have been quick work. The firing continues so that the smoke obscures all view. Then to my relief the sergeant-major comes along. He too is wondering what is going to happen and we wait together silently. Gradually the firing dies down. It ceases. We go back to my platoon and beyond to see Smalley on the right. He has put his men into their P.H. helmets, mistaking the smoke for a gas attack. "All's well that ends well." But we do not fail to chaff Smalley about his precaution.

Night in the trenches

Night has fallen. The stars shine brilliantly and (these trenches facing north) I gaze at The Plough dipping towards High Wood. What joy it is to know that you in England and I out here at least can look upon the same beauty in the sky! We've the stars to share. Look at them! They have become seers—images of divine stability—

guardians of a peace and order beyond the power of weak and petty madness. Upon what havoc and ruin have they looked down in days of Greece and Rome and centuries beyond! Still they shine and keep their calm serenity. They, at least, will outlast the war and still be beautiful. We cannot shoot the stars.

If only those two guns on the horizon beyond High Wood could stop! They flash a pair of devilish eyes and we, trembling, wait the result; for they are firing on us. Already they have knocked the trench in twice, luckily at unoccupied places. It's all because of that damned machine-gun that keeps hammering away on our left. Why on earth do they want to keep firing into the dark like that?

Hill and I think it our duty to find out. After some difficulty we discover the machine-gun and ask the gunners if they can't stop for a while. Sorry, but they've instructions to carry on over-head fire all night on a road beyond the hill which it is reported the Germans use every night.

We come back to my burrow and crawl in, drawing the ground-sheet across the opening so that we can strike a match and by the light of a candle eat and smoke.

This is the first time in the trenches for us both, and we marvel at the continuous shelling, wondering if it is ever going to stop. Hill falls asleep and with friendship's pity I look upon his sleeping face.

Then a whiz-bang bursts just above us and he wakes, scared like a child. We climb out and parade, for the rest of the night up and down the trench.

Dawn over Delville Wood

Morning breaks shrouded in mist: pale pink veils in the sky above announce the coming of the sun. We shall have seemed to have lived another day before the inhabitants of England awake. These hours between dawn and noon are the longest of the twenty-four. At home we breakfast at eight and try to cram in a day's work before six. Here we breakfast at four or five, and the clock goes round on leaden wheels over the hours of our enforced idleness: the day's work is never begun or ended.

The shelling goes on, now heaviest over Delville Wood. We go and look down over it, from the horseshoe bend in the trench on Smalley's right flank, as the mist begins to clear. We can only guess very roughly the lie of our own and the German trenches: not a living thing is to be seen. The wood itself is just a collection of stakes stuck upright in the ground, looking like the broken teeth of some vicious beast. Shells drop everywhere, making little Etnas as they burst, but we cannot tell which are the hits.

Shelling in trenches

I've a prescription for anyone who wants to know what being shelled in trenches is like. Here it is.

Dig a hole in the garden fairly close to the house, a few yards long, six feet deep and about four feet wide. At night go armed with a pop-gun and stand in this hole. Then persuade the members of your family to throw into the hole from the upper windows of the house every utensil and article of furniture they can lay hands on: crockery, fire-irons, coal, chairs, tables, beds, let them heave the lot at you, not forgetting the grand piano, just to give you an idea of a nine-inch shell. You must not leave the hole, but while the bombardment is going on you are quite at liberty to march up and down, eat, sleep, remove the débris that doesn't hit you, and generally to pretend that nothing unpleasant is happening. Remain there for a few days or you will evade the trench-dweller's worst enemy, boredom; and if you want to be realistic, add heat, shortage of water, stench, shortage of sleep, and give yourself the actual possibility of being killed every moment.

It would give some idea. Of course you would miss the noise. But you would know the sense of futility which being shelled in a trench produces. At the end of your "tour" I think you would understand how sage a comment on the experience was that made by a poor scared fellow I met on

Pommiers Redoubt. He had just come out of
trenches where most of his companions had been
killed by shelling and, looking at me with wide,
staring eyes, he said, "Why, this isn't war at all.
It's bloody murder!"

"A soft time"

We seem to have been here for weeks: actually
we have been here three days. It has been what
is called "a soft time," too, for the only casualties
in the battalion have occurred in the company behind us, and there they have only had about half
a dozen killed and wounded. We hear the batteries have suffered heavily, and small wonder, for
so far the shelling has never stopped.

This afternoon, frayed out with the incessant
noise, I went to see Rowley in his miserable little
dug-out for the sole purpose of asking him whether
shelling ever did stop. He smiled and inquired
what I expected, adding that it was "a bit steep,"
but we ought to be thinking ourselves damned
lucky we weren't getting it. I was immensely grateful to him, for he was friendly and not in the least
superior. I shall owe him something for that kindness as long as we are together.

Digging in front

As dark comes on we are filing out to dig a new
communication-trench down in the valley between
the front line and our own. Passing a dump, the

men draw picks and shovels alternately. It is strange and exciting to be in the open again. The men are extended in line while the tape is being laid. They begin to chatter—too loudly it seems, for half a dozen whiz-bangs come fizzing right among us, glaring red as they burst. The men flop, and I, knowing no better, do the same. Down along the line comes Rowley cursing the men furiously.

"What the hell do you think you are doing lying there?"

I get up feeling badly chagrined, and the work is begun. For a couple of hours it is continued, practically undisturbed. Then we file hurriedly back to the trench, learning as we enter it that we are to return to the work in the morning.

Half-wounded

Another perfect day; but against the blue sky beyond High Wood an observation-balloon hangs ominously. If we were shelled in the dark, how shall we fare in such daylight as this with that balloon hanging over there?

Anyway—merciful and delicious relief!—the shelling here has ceased at last.

At moments there is real silence. To our tired ears this absence of sound is positive and acute pleasure: we drink it like wine, loath to break it even with conversation.

Wondering what will happen, we file down the

hillside. To our surprise the silence continues. Out in the bright sunlight the trench is deepened and widened and not a shot is fired at us, though looking across the valley we can see shrapnel falling, ironically enough, on the trenches we have left.

Soon after noon we return, very hot, to eat our bully beef and bread, sitting on the firestep. Castlereagh, bright lad, has made me a drink of tea, which I am thankful to accept even from his mess-tin. But while drinking it, I feel a smack on the neck and look round to see who is throwing earth about. No one looks guilty, and putting my hand up I find my neck bleeding; and there at my feet lies an inch of shrapnel I had not seen before. Luckily it must have been the flat side that hit and split the skin. Hill ties me up and we laugh over our first "casualty." Then Rowley comes along and, brushing my ridicule aside, insists that I must report to the M.O. for anti-tetanus inoculation. I can get on at once with Hardy's sergeant, and afterwards, on behalf of the company, "take over" at Pommiers Redoubt where the battalion is due again to-night. We shall pass the dressing-station on the way out.

That greasy-looking M.O.! Rowley says that he covers his skin with the fat of bully beef to save washing and keep off the lice, and though that is probably gross libel, unfortunately it looks true. I suffer his attentions, wondering what devil of malice he must house to make him scornful of our

easy spell, and together the sergeant and I go into
the fearsome valley.

Suddenly those black-bursting shells known as
"coal-boxes" begin to fall. They come with terrifying explosions, and we scuttle in search of a
deep communication-trench there should be hereabouts. At the far end of the valley a limber is
moving along the road. A shell comes over, and
when the cloud of smoke clears, the wagon is gone
and the horses are bolting down the road. A moment later and we are mopping our hot faces in
the comparative security of the deep trench.

The doctor

My platoon arrives at the Redoubt as twilight
fades. The sergeant reports "all correct," except
that Brown, a youngster among the Gallipoli men,
is "bad." I find him lying on the ground breathing heavily and apparently unconscious. He should
not have been given that box of bombs to carry.
I loosen his tunic and try the ordinary restoratives
without effect. This is a case for the doctor. After
searching for some time, I find him at mess in the
Headquarters dug-out; so I send down a message.
He comes up, evidently annoyed at being dis-
turbed, and I apologise as we go to the boy together. The doctor bends over him for a moment,
and then, rising, shouts with astonishing fury:
"You damned young scrimshanker, get up! What

the devil do you fancy you're playing at? Think
you can swing the lead on me? Get up, or I'll have
you in the guard-room."

He pushes the boy with his foot, but the lad
does not stir.

"Don't you think he is ill?"

"Ill! There's nothing the matter with him at
all. Just 'wind up,' the bloody young coward.
Leave him there if he doesn't get up, and don't
call me again. I don't waste my time over these
damned scrimshankers."

He turns and goes back to the dug-out.

This strikes me as callous brutality, and for a
moment I am at a loss to know what to do. The
men around come to the rescue. They pick up the
boy, assuring me they will look after him. As they
carry him off I hear them murmuring, "Brute,"
"Swine."

"He had the fever in Gallipoli," the sergeant
explains, "and he gets these attacks. I think he'll
come to after a bit, and then we'll get him something warm."

During the next two months it is distressing to
watch this boy's efforts to carry on. With the help
of the sergeant-major, he is given all the easiest
jobs and most comfortable places available; but
the marching is always too much for him. He carries his pack like the burden of Atlas. In the end
he has a similar attack after a long march, and the

battalion having now changed doctors, I send
for the new M.O., who orders the boy to hospital
on the next day.

Still alive

It is marvellous to be out of the trenches: it is
like being born again. The cloud of uncertainty
that hung above us every moment while we were
under fire, putting its minatory query before the
least anticipation, is lifted, and we are free to say,
"In an hour's time," without challenging Fate with
the phrase. When freedom to anticipate is being
persistently challenged, one understands as never
before how much man lives by hope. To be de-
prived of reasonable expectation—even of the next
moment—is the real strain. I had not thought of
that. Certainty, even of violent death, would often
come as a relief. It is the perpetual uncertainty that
makes life in the trenches endurance all the time.
"Stick it" has become a password: intelligibly the
right one. We have to forget "I shall." It is this
constriction of hope that depresses men in the
trenches. "If" stands before every prospect, and
it is no small "if" in this war.

But here we are, alive again, like men redeemed
from the grave. We have left the trenches behind.

Instinctively we feel as if we have earned the
right to go home. We gave Death the chance.
Death did not take it and we've escaped alive.
What about it? Isn't the war finished—at least

for us? Some of these men have put their lives in pawn a hundred times. Haven't at least they earned the right of respite? Surely you who live walled round by safety would not demand of these men that they shall keep on offering Death their lives till he accepts? Surely, despite your grey hairs, you'd rather leap from seats of assembly and run into the breach yourselves? I hope you would, but now I am wondering whether you've imagination enough to know what's happening. I should like to remind army commanders, cabinet ministers and other members of parliament, that soldiers only respect those in command over them who are themselves willing to hazard their lives. Napoleon knew this. It behoves them to remember. If they are content merely to prescribe our fates, let them be assured that their share in the honours of posterity will be the award of contempt.

Anyway we are alive again for a time—most probably—though three men have been killed in a cook-house that was standing here when we left, but has since been shelled out of sight. Peace will come some day, bringing to some men, if not to us, its almost unthinkable reprieve. Peace might even come to-day. Who can tell?

Battle instructions
Peace has not arrived. On the contrary, I've just come from a meeting of officers before the C.O.,

at which he told us we are going back to make an attack from Orchard Trench.

He was needlessly emphatic about the word "Retire" and its deletion from our vocabulary. We haven't come out here to retire. Even so, if an officer did use the word, I doubt if we should obey that strict injunction to shoot him. We shan't win this war shooting one another. And all those details about battle police being appointed and instructed to shoot loiterers: are they necessary? Anyone would think we were criminal conscripts.

Alas for the old romantic pictures of the colonel leading his men into the fray! His last words to them now are these scarce-veiled threats.

If only the romantic British public knew! Yet, in the words of our battle-hymn, "They'd never believe it."

Under fire

Cheerio! "For it again," as we say. Here's the latest order:

Two half-companies under the command of two subalterns per half-company will report to the officer of the Royal Engineers for digging on the communication-trench at St. George's Hill this evening.

The lot has fallen on Smalley and me. My cut in the neck hardly pities me, but I would have dodged that inoculation had I known; for now, at the height of its effect, it produces headache and drowsiness.

We parade at dusk and trail back to the deep trench that Hardy's sergeant and I were glad to find yesterday afternoon. Here we stop and wait. An hour goes by; we are still waiting. At last word trickles down that there is heavy shelling on the trench we are bound for: we have been waiting for this to hold up. A little later we file along, and after much stumbling over wire and other obstructions come out near the old horseshoe bend.

What's all this confusion? Suddenly I see, silhouetted against the moonlit sky, the figure of a man borne high on the shoulders of stretcher-bearers. He is waving his arms and in a hoarse voice shouting and crying for water, like a man in a tragic melodrama. The bearers tell him to be quiet and lie down, but he takes no notice of them, and as we pass I see blood half covers his face. Round the corner of the trench a boy sits moaning. "He wants his mother," whispers the man tending him. "He's been hit in the stomach." The boy gives a sigh and dies as we pass.

We stumble on down the valley and into the shallow trench. All is quiet now. Smalley and I run along the top, setting out the men about a couple of yards apart. The engineer officer comes along and courteously asks me if I will please count the men in the trench. I have nearly finished when a machine-gun out of High Wood starts firing on

us. I jump into the trench among the men. It is
not more than two feet deep, and we have to
lie flat, for the gun is traversing and the bullets
mow like a scythe. The earth drops on our faces
as the stroke passes and again as the sweep returns. The man at my head is in mortal terror.
"They're coming over! They're coming over! My
God! We're for it now!" The man at my feet is
perfectly cool. "Jerry's got the wind up," he remarks slowly. "I reckon he's got the wind up,
don't you, sir? He needn't fret himself." For my
part, I wish my heart would stop thumping.

The machine-guns have not ceased before shelling begins. That at least means they are not coming over yet; but to be shelled in a bit of a ditch
like this is terrifying. Over and over they come,
now short, now beyond, now so close a red glare
fills the eyes and a wave of heat scorches the face.
This lasts about ten minutes, and as it dies down,
the machine-guns begin again, sweeping the top of
the trench with fiendish accuracy. Now, worse than
all, heavy shells are dropping. Crump! Boom!
Thud! The storm rises to its height with shells of
all calibres. On and on—light, heat and sound, in
agonising confusion. This surely must be the end.
I suffer the last torment of fear, and then, as one
who has already passed through the gate, concen-
trate every faculty in the effort to focus life to this
point. I am ready; but Death fails to come. To
my surprise the moments lengthen: the firing

begins to die down. Like a sick man coming out
of delirium I hear it growing less and less. It stops.
I am amazedly alive.

We get on our feet; but the men of the battalion
posted farther up the trench, frightened by their
casualties and swearing in their fear, come blun-
dering past, pushing and tearing their way out
of the trench. As soon as they have passed we
begin to dig, but we have not been at work long
before the engineer comes up, and after thanking
us with the same courtesy, tells us we may go.

The men assemble on the hill, excited and
pleased with their luck. We hurry away, and in
our haste miss the communication-trench. A cold
mist comes down making the task of finding it in
the dark impossible. We wander on through the
night seeking the way; the men are apparently
too glad to be alive to complain. Morning breaks
cold and dank, when we at last discover the
plateau.

Brunning sits down

Another reprieve. The attack is not coming
off. We are going right out, to come back in another part of the line. What luck! Now we shall
get letters.

I've just met Brunning, who was with B half-
company last night. It appears he was blown up,
but came down again, sitting. Being fat he suffered
no damage beyond bruises. To-day he waddles like

a duck, for the first time in his life cannot see the joke; which is not surprising, seeing where the point of it lies.

It's just what would happen to Brunning.

Lice

This morning I slept in a big German dug-out to which Rowley had moved while Smalley and I were out last night. It would have been wiser to have slept on top, for that filthy old place has left me a legacy of lice. People at home are horrified at the thought of lice, but they seem a very minor ill here. Apparently no one who sees much of the front line is altogether free from them. They are a curse when the body becomes heated. New underclothing seems the best remedy; which means that men must suffer more than officers in this respect, as they undoubtedly do in many other more serious ways.

On the march

We are on the march, now twenty miles from the line as the crow flies, making for the little village of Bonniers, about eight miles north-east of Doullens. We returned by the road we had come, as far as Méricourt, bivouacking again at Belle Vue Farm, and stopping for a couple of days at the old chalk hillside near Dernancourt. From Méricourt we trained to Candas, and since then have been making zig-zag tracks about the country, presumably to get out of the way of troops going up to the trenches. Last night we stopped at le Meillard.

It is good to leave the guns behind and get back to the comparative quiet of these long white roads, lined with tall trees. The country is mildly picturesque, and now everywhere one sees the French peasant at work on his harvest. He is usually an old man and most of his helpers are women; but he is getting the work done—the solid, satisfactory, primary work of harvesting the grain. On the road outside the farmhouse stands the thresher. The sound of threshing is good music. I could listen to it and watch the corn falling into the hopper for half the day. As we march past the peasants scarcely trouble to raise their eyes; they have probably seen too many of our kind already. We are intruders upon their work; however necessary just now, still intruders.

We are marching as a brigade, and strict march discipline is observed. Each regiment of the four takes its turn at the head of the column; and no small difference does it make on dusty roads whether you happen to be at the head or the tail of the column: not merely (as the uninitiated might imagine) because of the dust, but chiefly because of the concertina movement between the files that almost inevitably occurs when a large body of men marches over an undulating surface. Bad marching increases the amount of this "play," till the men in the rear seem to be running and halting by turns; but even with the best going, since men are not automata, those at the tail of a column always feel they have farther to go.

For this reason one's chief duty, as a platoon commander on the march, is to see that the men keep properly closed up, taking no more than their correct amount of road-space either way. We halt regularly for ten minutes every hour, and "fall out" on the side of the road to rest and adjust our burdens. No drinking is allowed except by order. If a man falls out on the march without orders, or is guilty of any other breach of discipline, he is called to account on the following morning, and usually gets some extra duty by way of punishment, such as extra guard, or digging latrines with the pioneers.

At present we have no band: not only the bandsmen but the instruments were lost on July 1st. However, I hear the colonel is keen to raise something in the drum-and-fife line, and the men will welcome it, first with jeers and then with cheers, like every innovation. They whistle and sing anything but *Tipperary,* which, I suppose, died out here at Mons. Every now and then a strange song crops up with a local dialect, sometimes bawdy in its details; but that is by way of variety, when the platoon humorist happens to feel fresh. Our regular repertory is made up of last year's musical comedy with *I want to go*

Home, The Long Trail, Tennessee, and hymn-
tune parodies. They love the "sob stuff," and
roar out those inexplicable lines,

> *And roses round the door*
> *Make me love mother more*

(they sing "makes") with fervent gusto. When
singing dies down and there's no more whistling,
one knows they are tired or coming under fire.

At Bonniers

This old farmhouse is a very comfortable billet.
It stands in a shady lane under huge walnut-trees,
as if it had slept for centuries. The woman of the
house, too, is very agreeable, and last night cooked
us a delicious dish of omelets. Rumour says we are
staying awhile. I hope it is true. I should like an
hour or two to write letters. Hardy reads six-
penny novels. I envy him, for all literature seems
to me like a voice from another planet—desirable
and beautiful perhaps, but like an echo from the
farthest horizon. Hardy can even read while Rowley discusses sex.

There were some ugly feet at my parade for
foot inspection this evening—another reason why
I hope we shall stay for a bit. These fellows seem
to have a very elementary idea of how to look
after their feet. Since "sore feet" is an ill that
can be avoided, I am keen on these parades and
insist on regular washing, which surprises and

even amuses some men. Still, they are beginning to appreciate my administrations from the grease-pot. How a man can march with the flesh raw on his heel, like Bowler's, I can't imagine. I will get some spare socks sent out.

Going east again

Companies will parade on the road facing H.Q. in full marching order at 8.30 a.m.

This "chit" from the orderly room came round to Rowley at midnight. Here, indeed, we have no abiding city, and if we seek one to come, its name is never known to subalterns or men. We breakfast while in the same room the servants pack our valises, Castlereagh creating his own merry din over a strap he fancies someone has stolen. Belts are cleaned, tin hats found, and we hustle on to parade to find the men drawn up. The sergeant reports "all present and correct," and by nine we are on the move again, back along the road by which we came here yesterday.

It is a glorious morning, dew is still heavy on the ground, and the air is clear under a cloudless sky. Our first halt is by a wooded bank on the outskirts of Frohen-le-Grand—an idyllic spot with a stream running down one side of the road. Frohen itself is a charming place.

Now we take the road through Mézerolles to Doullens. It rises and falls along the north bank

of the River Authie that is sometimes hidden by
thick foliage and sometimes the foreground to
an enchanting wooded landscape. This constantly
changing scene makes the march go easily to me,
but some of the men are beginning to find the
heat oppressive. We halt just before Doullens,
and then proceed to clatter through the town.
After the trenches and the many villages we have
passed through, Doullens has the air of a city,
with its cobbled stones, large public buildings and
many civilians. Now we turn into what appears
to be a manufacturing quarter of the town, and
are ascending the steep hill on the eastern side.
The dust hangs in a cloud about the rear of the
battalion, and it is hard work to keep some of
the men going. Their rifles have to be carried for
them, and still they seem distressed. The songs
have ceased, and complaints come down from the
colonel about spreading over the road. Frayed
and hot, we make the top of the hill and pull ourselves together for a last lap. A couple of miles on
we turn sharp to the right and descend the hill
leading to Halloy.

It has not been a long march, only sixteen miles,
but in the ranks, on a hot day, with several days'
marching behind you, with forty pounds on your
back and a long column in front, it wants endurance. 'Tis easier to do twice the distance under
civil conditions.

Some portraits

> *All places that the eye of heaven visits*
> *Are to a wise man ports and happy havens.*

This orchard on the outskirts of Halloy is certainly one. While the eye of heaven looks down upon these flimsy canvas shelters in the orchard, their simple accommodation is very pleasant. We might be camping out in a country garden. Officers have primitive beds of canvas stretched over rough frames. The men sleep on the ground, but there is plenty of room and I should think they prefer those quarters to the barn, stable, or forsaken and dilapidated room they usually get for a billet.

Halloy has evidently been used as a rest-camp for some time. It has a town-major. A town-major is a kind of military mayor whose duty it is to regulate the occupation, sanitation and general economy of the place. Town-majorship is usually held by an officer of the rank of captain, and is regarded as a safe and comfortable job, though it must be full of petty annoyances, for he is the disposer of billets and has to mediate between the natural wishes of the inhabitants of the town and military requirements.

Taylor, a captain who had one of the companies before the 1st of July, has returned to the battalion and taken over the adjutancy. He is a tall, lean, well-educated man, with a superficial ease and grace of manner that must be welcome to hostesses. A perfect diplomat, his stimulated vivacity in the presence of his superiors leaves him at other times with that look of weariness so typical of the tactician. I see him as a slave of the desire to please, and even while I despise him for it, feel an innate sympathy with him.

He sits at the far end of this shelter, drinking with Rowley and Simpkins of D Company. He drinks a lot, fidgeting all the time. Obviously his nerve has gone.

Simpkins is the fool-who-knows-his-job type of officer. Short and heavy featured, he has the colourless air of one whose intelligence never reaches the study of human nature. He jokes like a hippopotamus; wakes to vitality in the presence of the colonel, but shows a dull, boorish eye to subalterns and men. They say the interior economy of his company is the best in the battalion. I wonder now whether, as a fighting unit, he is preferable to the no-fool-who-doesn't-know-his-job type—the type one so often met among the stray Jews at the training-camps in England? Maybe; but there's a lot wanting in a commander of men who is without intuition.

Wilson of A Company is the shining light among the captains. He is about forty-five: a short, red, fair man with eyes that twinkle under long brows, a gentle paternal manner and a secret well of good spirits that quietly bubbles over. A very strict disciplinarian, I should think he might have been a schoolmaster. His wrath is fiery and short-lived: his discipline effective, because he seems to insist upon it as though it were a form of natural good manners that had social service and amenity for its end, and not a tyranny that is an end in itself. Wilson is no prig, but I wonder whether his subalterns do not find the paternal air a little oppressive. Anyway, it is obvious that the men have respect and affection for him. Men are lynx-eyed for character.

Lilley of B is the dandy of the regiment. With his dark curly hair and apple complexion, he is a regular Adonis. His name suits him too well. The war becomes a vulgarity at the sight of Lilley —all this disorder around a perfectly-turned-out specimen of English good-looks; and in a Cromwellian tin hat, too, that looks ridiculous on the head of one who is obviously a cavalier born out of his time. He is much too well-bred and handsome for this ugly war, and ought to be given a job at the War Office. Just to see him marching down the Mall would be an encouragement to the folks at home.

Meanwhile those three at the end of the shelter are getting to the bottom of the whisky-bottle. Their conversation is not edifying: that old rascal Rowley sees to that.

Sailly-au-Bois

We have reached the deserted village of Sailly-au-Bois, three miles behind the line at Hébuterne.

The men are in cellars of the forsaken houses, for the place is shelled occasionally. Our company headquarters is an imposing farmhouse that stands back from the road, walled-in, with a large clean cobbled courtyard in front. It has a cellar we can hop into in case of trouble, but we prefer to sleep on the ground-floor where there are still one or two pieces of furniture. A six-inch gun hides in the orchard at the back, firing rarely.

On the march yesterday we halted at Souastre, turning into a field that lay in a hollow where the field-kitchens were got to work cooking us a meal. While we were thinking about moving off again, shells began to drop in the town. They came as a great surprise, for the place had not been shelled for weeks, and gave us a sharp reminder of our whereabouts. Thence on to Sailly the cloud of apprehension seemed to hang over us, making the men quiet and producing the unmistakable signs of tension. Now we shall live under that cloud more or less consciously for—how long?

The post-boy

Shells have been dropping in the village. Going out to see that all was well with my little crowd, I met the company post-boy, who has been in France for over a year. He was looking white but extraordinarily pleased. His right hand was bound up and his arm was in a sling. A shell dropped on the road while he was going his round with the letters, and before he could find cover he had lost a couple of fingers. That finishes the war for him. He knows it, and his delight is undisguised. He will start for England when we start for the trenches this afternoon. I envy him keenly, but my envy is mixed with a peculiar pleasure at the thought that this boy, now actually here, will form a link between us and the land of heart's desire. I could make garlands for him to take back.

Hébuterne

We are going in by platoons. Hardy and Hill have already moved off. We are waiting our five minutes' interval under the trees that arch over the road. Time's up. "Number eleven platoon! 'Shun! Slope 'ipe! Form fours! Right! By the right, quick march!" The shortest way to the line would be by the road, but it is under observation of the enemy from the rising ground at Gomme-court, so we pass through a gap in the trees and take the open track across fields that two years ago grew corn. The detour is just sufficient to hide us, but the fields lie open as a plain the whole way to Hébuterne. We keep Hill's platoon in sight, following it for half an hour until it disappears in the village. As we enter the village we come upon the ruined church. The roof has gone and the near wall leans over us at a perilous angle; yet within we can see images still standing on the altar. Beyond the shadow of the church we face the main street of the village which we enter, turning sharp to the right. Here we keep to the middle of the road to avoid falling masonry in case of shelling. Although knocked about, the houses stand in recognisable order, and we wonder as we pass them by whether they are beyond repair. Near the end of the village we turn suddenly to the left and dive into an old communication-trench. It winds on interminably by the foundations of houses and through the village gardens, its walls moss-grown and worn, its floor often bricked. This brings us out at last into a maze of trenches that has been in regular occupation for a year. Until recently they were held by the French, who seem to have had a taste for a quiet life and a good idea of making themselves comfortable.

The troops we are relieving are Scots whose kilts make a welcome spot of colour in the drab trench. They hand over in a leisurely manner that is very agreeable and show us just how they have held the line, telling us that this has been a quiet front since the 1st of July, when they buried half a battalion of men in a front-line trench that has been abandoned.

Ours is the second line. A and B Companies are about a hundred yards in front. D is in reserve, occupying cellars of houses on the eastern outskirts of the town. We have a long winding sector of trench, revetted here and there with fine wire, and again in many places floored with bricks. There are no bays, so we post the men at various firing-points at fairly wide intervals and put Lewis gunners out on both flanks. Other disused trenches wind about in the rear of our line, and altogether there appear to be many opportunities for losing one's way and finding that extraordinary and sometimes terrifying loneliness which solitude in the trenches can beget.

What impresses me now, as I seek the company dug-out, is the amazing quiet. Not only is there little or no shelling here, but during the last five minutes I have heard nothing but the distant rumble of guns far down on the Somme. Blessed relief! Long may it continue. Was it Ruskin who said that the upper and more glorious half of Nature's pageant goes unseen by the majority of people? Eulogising Turner's skies, I think he said something of the kind. Well, the trenches have altered that. Shutting off the landscape, they compel us to observe the sky; and when it is a canopy of blue flecked with white clouds like this, and when the earth below is a shell-stricken waste, one looks up with delight, recalling perhaps the days when, as a small boy, one lay on the garden lawn at home counting the clouds as they passed.

Rats

Our dug-out is not very deep, but it's a wonder-ful place. At the bottom of the steps on the left there are two canvas bunks that are extremely comfortable when you have walked up and down the trench for an hour or two. Then there's a table, which Rowley naturally monopolises, and a chair, which is also Rowley's. But that's not all. Marvel of marvels, there's a great gilt mirror, big enough to reflect two or even three shaving faces at the same time. All this makes for luxury; but there's one fly in the ointment, apart from lice, of which the old place has its complement. I refer to rats.

Rats outside I saw last night at twilight. They were squeaking and gibbering all over the rough ground of the cast-up earth, and Hill and I have wasted a good supply of revolver ammunition potting at them. Twice during the night I trod on them in the trench, and just now, as I was lying in this top bunk, I noticed the strip of sack-ing that serves as ceiling, blobbing about, and promptly kicked the blobs into quietness. But the war on rats is being prosecuted with the fiercest determination, as they say, in the ante-room to this chamber, where the orderlies keep their gear.

Smalley sits on the chair reversed with his re-volver pointed over the back. He is looking in-tently along the sights and his aim is at a large rat-hole. On the other side Rowley also stands

armed, ready for general emergencies. The main
drama, however, rests between his servant and
Smalley's, one of whom holds against the wall
a large piece of cheese on the end of a bayonet,
while the other stands "on guard," his bayonet
fixed, ready to make the movements "in" and
"out," as on parade, at the first appearance of
the rat. Already two corpses testify to the efficiency of the bayonet as a weapon of war.

Routine and gas

How unmercifully slowly the days wear away!
Just before dawn the order "stand to" comes
round, and then everybody is wakened, bayonets
are fixed, Rowley comes out of the dug-out, followed by the subalterns who happened to be sleeping at the time, and in the chilly air we watch the
sunrise. Looking east, we have the advantage of
the Germans at dawn. I only wish both sides
would agree to sing hymns to the sun, for the
beauty of these autumn sunrises is very great, and
it seems a pity to leave their celebration to artil-
lerymen a mile or so behind, who come out and
pop off a few rounds for our benefit before going
back to sleep.

As soon as the sun has risen we "stand down,"
only those who were sentries keeping to their
posts: the rest go to sleep again or have an in-
formal meal. Rowley returns to the dug-out to
write his report, which always includes news of

the wind's direction. At about seven the sergeant sends a couple of men out of the trenches to bring in dixies of hot tea from the field-kitchens which cook for us in the village; and these men go again for dinner at twelve, and again at four for more tea. In the middle of the morning a dozen or so 5.9 shells come over at regular half-minute intervals, and then the front nearly always remains quiet until "stand to" at sunset, when there's generally some rifle-firing and a machine-gun in Gommecourt shows us what it can do. Desultory firing goes on till midnight, when the place is quiet as a grave.

Now to-night, if the wind is favourable, gas is going over from our front line immediately after "stand to"; or, as Rowley informed us, "We are going to give the Huns a dose of their own bloody physic to-night. Let's hope it wipes out all the b—— in the trench."

"Let's hope it's not blown back," says Hardy, who has suffered gas at St. Julien.

We stand in the dark awaiting the effect.

Gas! I believe there's not a man among us, Rowley most certainly included, who does not feel some shamefacedness at this loathly method of war. Many times since I heard the news I have said to myself, "They started it." I wonder why I find it necessary to say it to myself so many times?

It is half-past nine. If the gas went off to time

it should have reached them now. Yes, the machine-guns have begun to rattle, and there is a fusillade of rifle-fire. A rain of bullets sings above us, spattering among the trees that over-hang this trench. It behoves us to keep our heads down. For about an hour this rapid fire is kept up, and the village is treated to a few extra shells which reverberate among the houses behind us. Then all is normal again, and we are left with a sickly wondering what has happened in the German line.

Coming out

All is a bustle and stir in the trench. We are being relieved. Except that Barlow has lost his mess-tin and Smith his ground-sheet, we are ready to move off; but before we are free to go we must show patience to the incoming troops and answer every question the merest lancejack may ask about how the line is held. They are fairly satisfied at last, and we clutter along the tortuous communication-trench, moving at about double the pace we made coming in. Out on the main street the men slip into fours without any need for hustling, and there are no complaints from rear files about the pace, however much those in front step out. Striding along, one feels a tremor run through the little band at the sound of shells falling behind us; but the pace does not alter. We are coming out. Every step is one nearer that invisible, yet instinctively appreciable line which marks the danger zone. As we round the church corner breath comes bated, for there were casualties here this morning, and it is a critical spot. We are passing. . . . We are by. . . . Another of Death's gins and traps escaped. Now for the plain! The pace is kept going: indeed needs checking; for we must keep our distance from the platoon in front. On we go. Somebody begins to whistle and the tune is quickly caught up: the spirit of gaiety is beginning to loosen its wings. Through Hébuterne, past the old billets, and now up the hill on the road to Bayencourt. Singing breaks out as we make the top of the hill. We are beyond the palsied area: almost to a yard this is where we cross the line. The cloud of foreboding is lifted: the expectation of life is free and natural again.

Quartermasters

We have been staying at Bayencourt four days: the men billeted in rooms down the village. We officers are at a starveling farm just outside. A French peasant and his wife were still in possession on our arrival and were much aggrieved at being ejected; but I suppose military necessity knows no law.

This afternoon I took my platoon down to the quartermaster's stores while Rowley was saying farewell to the doctor over a bottle of whisky. Thank Heaven, *he* is going. I hear he fell out

with the colonel. It is certainly probable, because
a battalion only wants one commander at a time.

I suppose we did fairly well down at the stores,
but until I was commissioned, I little knew how
much that important item of a junior officer's
duty, "the care of his men," depends for its successful accomplishment upon the temper of the
quartermaster and the subaltern's ability to keep
on the right side of it. Quartermasters are queer
fish. In the first place, their status is peculiar because, though it is above non-commissioned and
below ordinary commissioned rank, they reign
supreme in their own department. As a class they
may be described as "hard-faced." Then their
job is a most complicated and all-embracing one.
In practice a quartermaster is butcher, baker,
grocer, ready-made clothes dealer, accountant, de-
tective, universal provider and charity organisation agent; and it all depends on the quartermaster whether you are wise to approach him
on the business or the charitable side. Most quartermasters seem to prefer the latter, and since,
if you insist upon military and commercial rights,
you may find yourself having to appeal to high
tribunals with expert evidence in opposition, a
wise subaltern falls out with the quartermaster
only in the last extremity. This is sometimes gall-
ing, for, as I said, quartermasters on the whole
are hard-faced men, inclined to act upon the as-
sumption that the ideal quartermaster is he who

can retain his goods on the shop side of the counter for all eternity. If a Socialistic state meant the universal appointment of quartermasters, I should turn vegetarian and wear the garb of Adam. I could not face that music on my own behalf.

Back at Hébuterne

We are in the front line at Hébuterne, just a little to the right of the trenches the battalion held last time. Fusiliers are on our right flank; D Company on our left. The ground to our front slopes gently away for a few hundred yards, and then rises again in a long sweep. Slightly to our right we can just see the white tower of the church in Achiet-le-Petit, half-hidden by trees. To our left, standing on slightly higher ground and almost enfilading us, is Gommecourt, a sinister spot, now a heap of rubble and the bare remnants of a wood. All day it reveals no sign of life, but under cover of darkness it becomes a venomous beast, spitting machine-gun fire. On our extreme right the ground falls away. Down in that near hollow stand the three poplars where it is reported the Germans are sapping. Beyond lies the valley overlooking Serre, and in the far distance Beaumont-Hamel. The German trenches are just behind the long roll of barbed wire that stands like a wave a hundred yards away. Those forsaken trenches, a few paces in front of us, are the graves

of many of the men who held this bit of line
prior to July 1st.

The lovely weather still holds: we have come
to take it for granted; but the preparations now
being made in this trench show foresight of coming rain. It rather looks as if the higher command
had decided to hold on here for the winter.
Engineers are busy on two deep dug-outs that will
each be capable of accommodating half a company, and the Tunnelling Corps is secretly very
busy laying a mine—to blow up Gommecourt, we
hope. In the trench itself, revetting with wire and
sandbags is systematically going on, and the floor
is being drained and covered with new duck-
boards, not only up here, but right down the communication-trench to the second line. Altogether
these trenches offer the sharpest contrast to the
rough bayless chasm of St. George's Hill, or even
the comparatively formless second line we occupied last week. These must be after the pattern
of the routine trench-warfare of 1915. We
brought rolls of barbed wire and bundles of sandbags in with us, and to-night we shall begin our
share of the improvements.

SEPTEMBER

SEPTEMBER

Wiring

$\mathcal{S}$MALLEY AND I ARE ON TOP WITH a wiring-party. Queer and eerie the sensation of standing high above the heads of Germans in the trench just over there beyond the wire. With automatic regularity they keep firing Verey lights that rise like roman candles and reveal our silhouetted forms to one another so clearly it seems impossible at first to believe the enemy cannot see us. When the light is strong we stand stock-still. At first these moments are terrifying; then, as time goes on, one gains confidence in the darkness that covers our own trenches. Just now I was badly scared by a light that seemed to come right out of no-man's land, just behind my back. Luckily I dropped in a shell-hole before the light began to fall.

One cannot realise how hideously ploughed up this ground is till one begins to wander about over it. It is simply a succession of larger and smaller shell-holes. What a fearful job it must be to keep men in an attack, over such ground, in any sort of regular formation! Here, slowly wiring, it is simply devilish difficult to get alignment, and one takes a fantastic time getting from place to place. If we didn't live in momentary fear of those machine-guns suddenly starting again out of Gommecourt, the efforts of some of these fellows would be comic. As it is, it is infuriating to find one man tying himself up in his own strand of wire and another going pell-mell down a deep shell-hole; or to hear two fools cursing each other in loud tones that will give us away if they are not silenced.

We wire badly. I must ask Rowley for wiring practice next time we are out of the line.

A "dud" sergeant

I have twenty men with my sergeant pushing forward a bombing-post under cover of night. Getting out on top, I set the men at their proper intervals in the trench and stand by for a while before handing over to the sergeant. Coming back I find him lolling against the wall of the front-line trench, idly talking to Corporal Neal. Not seeing me, he continues this for some time; so I fetch him out on top, take him to the head of the sap and leave him there. Half an hour afterwards I go back to find him sitting where I left him, only now fast asleep. One would have thought that for the sake of his own skin he would have at least remained awake. If a raiding party came over they would come on him first. Ignorant, insensitive, snoring lump—let him stay there. Of course

I ought to haul him up before the C.O., and perhaps get him shot for sleeping on duty. But what's
the good? Besides, I don't want the trouble, especially as I hear his predecessor is rejoining the
battalion to take the worthless beggar's place.

Watching the shells

The outstanding feature of this kind of warfare
is that, practically speaking, one never sees the
enemy. We know by his effects that he is there,
but during more than half the day, if his trenches
were empty and he himself a myth, 'twould be
all the same. The exception proves the rule, and
I am reminded of this by the two Germans I saw
in the distance this afternoon digging and moving
about on the slope behind their line. Their appearance was regarded as an impertinence asking for
target practice which promptly followed. It was
probably off the mark, but good enough to make
them quickly disappear. They are the first living
Germans I have seen beyond no-man's land.

Looking over the top soon afterwards I saw
what struck me as a truly awful sight. One of
our guns was firing on the German front line. I
happened to be standing in the direct line of fire,
so that I could actually see the shell in the air
at the instant before it dived into the trench.
Stated thus, this doesn't sound very terrible; and
yet to watch the actual devil of destruction on
its way, hurtling through the air so that it ap-

peared like a black cricket-ball seen in its flight
for the thousandth part of a second, was to me
the most awful sight I've yet seen. Instinctively
one contrasted the force and velocity of the thing
with the human bodies it was making for.

Barrage-fire at Serre

The rumble on our right this afternoon is in-
creasing. Looking southward over the valley towards Serre we see shells bursting in rapid succession at the foot of a promontory. Like an on-
coming thunderstorm the rumble increases, now
rising to a roar, while the individual shell-bursts
become merged in a white line that moves slowly
forward like the smoke of a forest fire. A living
thing, it creeps on and on, up the side of the hill
and over the crest, to the accompaniment of a
sound like continuous thunder. In addition to the
barrage, big shells now fall behind it, making
volcanoes of earth. One thinks of the fate of
Sodom and Gomorrah and wonders whether it
could compare with this. From start to finish the
bombardment lasts fully half an hour; and then, as
we look over the stricken, still smouldering land,
we wonder what has happened. We shall never
know. No one, except those immediately concerned, will ever know. As we turn away, our
hearts go out to the poor devils who had to sit
under that fire.

Aeroplanes at sunset

As well as in their appearance, the aeroplanes are like the birds in their habits; for as birds sing at twilight and at dawn, so is the habitual singing of aeroplanes. Late in the afternoon we look back to see a squadron coming out of the sunset. Like rooks against the light they appear, gradually taking shape as the hum of their engines is heard rising and falling on the breeze. Nearer and nearer they come, till they whirl and manœuvre overhead, remaining for perhaps ten or fifteen minutes, and then, like a flock of homing birds, back they go into the fading sunlight. They take one's desire with them, for their pilots will sleep in sound beds to-night. Man has gone to his home at dusk for so many centuries, the habit has become an instinct. Staying here, we need resolution to break that instinct every time darkness descends.

Sleeping on duty

Day and night (unless patrols or working-parties are out in front) we have three men to every bay: one on sentry while the other two rest or sleep. The sergeant changes the sentries every hour. During the day the sentry's chief duty here is to keep his eye on the periscope and report any movement or change in the picture he sees there. At night he stands on the firestep and peers into the darkness over the top, his bayonet fixed and

his rifle always in his hand. Firing the Verey pistol
at night is nominally the privilege of the company-
sergeant-major; but at present our pistol won't
act, the only cartridges to be obtained don't fit it,
so we dispense with Verey lights. It seems to be a
matter of no account, for the Germans keep firing
enough for both sides. There are Lewis-gunners
and bombers at the head of one bombing-post,
and Corporal Jackson is in charge of another.
Odd the way that man always seems to be the
first in the trenches and the last out. I noticed, too,
that directly we get into the trenches his nonchalant air disappears and he becomes keen on
whatever job falls to him. When I went to see
him just now, he told me in his piping, far-away
voice exactly how he was holding the post and
what he should do if there was any trouble, showing clearly that he had worked the whole situation out for himself. He is my best N.C.O.

At night the men seem to like being visited.
The most taciturn in daylight will talk at night.
Up till twelve o'clock I prefer night to day duty.
Turning out in the very early hours is not exactly
pleasant; but as each subaltern only does four
hours at a time, it is never very arduous. The
sergeant called me up an hour ago and we went
round once together. Now I have dispensed with
him; 'tis so seldom one can be alone out here.

Old Burt, the bruiser, looked funny when I
passed him; I think I'll go back and make sure

he's awake. There he is, and it certainly doesn't look like it. His head rests on his chest and his rifle is leaning against the corner of the bay. The other two men are sprawled on the firestep, sleeping. No, Burt, this won't do!

Quietly I collect all three rifles, hide them in the traverse and get up on the firestep beside Burt. Still he does not wake. Burt, my man, you must have a lesson. I load my revolver and fire it over the top, almost in the man's ear, shouting "Hands up!" All three jump to their feet feeling for their rifles and fairly gibbering with fear. There follows a short and vehement address. I return them their rifles and, pointing an obvious moral, leave them.

Somehow the scene when they awoke was too pitiable and realistic to be amusing; but I don't think Burt will sleep on sentry again. I wonder if he thinks I shall split on him?

Corporal Side

"What is the life of man! Is it not to shift from side to side?—from sorrow to sorrow?—to button up one cause of vexation—and unbutton another?"

Side has lost his kit. A 5.9 dropped in his trench, while he was absent upon a business essential to health, and demolished the bay together with all Corporal Side's worldly effects in France. He is much aggrieved. I met him round the bend.

"I hear you've had a lucky escape," I remarked.

"The beggars 'a got all my kit," he replied lugubriously.

The good fortune of being alive seemed to have escaped his notice, perhaps because he has experienced it so often.

Side is a remarkable soldier. He looks less like a soldier than any man I have seen in France, and that is saying a good deal. He is short, cross-eyed, bandy-legged, and has a preference for boots and clothes sizes too big for him. In civil life I believe he is a rag-picker, and the character of his profession adheres, as it will, to the man. He joined the battalion two years ago as a stretcher-bearer, and on the 1st of July carried stretchers *under fire continuously* for twenty-four hours. Anyone who knows the weight of a loaded stretcher and remembers the heat, the condition of the ground, and what the firing was like upon that day, will agree with me that the Victoria Cross would have expressed rather less than Side's deserts. However, he for his bravery was promoted to full corporal in the fighting-ranks.

For parade purposes he really ought to be smuggled among the cooks: he would move any inspecting officer to fury. But in the trenches Side is a treasure. He is tireless and has the heart of a lion. The other day, when we were in the sap and shells were dropping uncomfortably near, some timid idiot set the rumour running that the Germans were coming over. I was standing close to Side when it reached him. "Coming over, are they?" he replied. " 'Ere, gimme my rifle," and before one could say "knife" he was gone up the sap, apparently intending to put the Germans back in their places single-handed.

Yes, Side is not much to look at, but he has hold of what may be called the business end of the war.

The Major

This place is beginning to show what the newspapers describe as "a certain amount of liveliness." (Why "liveliness"? Deathliness would be truer.) We are not accustomed to much shelling in the morning, but we have been watching shells fall between us and the second line for some time now.

We are still watching the bursts when who should appear round the bay of the trench but our second-in-command, Major Smythe! This is a great shock, for though Major Smythe looms very large on parade, I have never seen him in the trenches before. Out on rest he glows like a star of the first magnitude, making woe betide those who are ignorant of ceremonial behaviour; but he seems to suffer the fate of waning by exact degrees according to our proximity to the Germans. So well is this declension calculated that the star is reputed to suffer regular and complete eclipse, under cover of "officer-in-charge of the rear party," whenever the battalion is actually in trenches.

But here he is, showing Rumour in her old colours; and how friendly he is as he invites me upon a tour of inspection! I respond cordially; but he seems to be in rather a hurry—indeed, before I can show him how the land lies, he has vanished round the next bay. I follow, and he does the vanishing trick again. It really becomes hard work to keep up: who'd have believed he could move so fast? Our "tour" degenerates at last into a walking-match, and I finish a bad second by the time he reaches the dug-out in the second line. Well, well! 'Tis true the trenches are no place for valuable lives, and Major Smythe, tall and thin, bears strong physical resemblance to Wellington. Perhaps he will play the great Duke reviewing his troops for the cinema—*après la guerre*.

Lieutenant Hardy

A boy in Hardy's platoon has just been killed. Hardy is upset. The boy was a chubby-faced youngster and something of a wag: not much younger than Hardy himself and always ready to have his leg pulled. He was standing in a bit of the trench that can be observed out of Gommecourt, and a whiz-bang fell at his feet, killing him instantly. Hardy has gone off to find the padre, and is very anxious the lad should be properly buried. I didn't know we had a padre, but it appears there's one attached to the brigade. Personally I should never have dreamt of seeking him now, but Hardy has great respect for the conventions; moreover, his feeling about decent burial is strong. His own, almost his only, fear for himself is lest his corpse should be left unburied. He told me the other day he simply could not stand the thought of his body being left on the wire to rot, and he extracted a promise from me to do what I could if he were killed. I made no compact with him, for I don't share his feeling, having too much concern for my living body to care what happens to it dead.

Hardy is too much of a child in many ways to make an ideal subaltern. He has what I consider a schoolboy's idea of discipline, and we rag one another on that score pretty regularly. But for pluck he is not to be beaten. If there's danger about, Hardy at once considers it his duty to be there, and he is reckless to a fault. The public-school tradition stands him in good stead, and he is an excellent example of its merits and limitations. The man who is brave by nature appraises the danger and then goes calmly into it. There is no calmness about Hardy; he can be easily scared out of his wits, wherein he shows the limitations of education by example; but where I admire him unfeignedly, and where the merits of the public-school system tell, is in the fact that being scared makes no difference to him. He is just as ready and full of pluck next time.

I find one grows to love and hate men here according as one feels that in crucial moments they will be on the spot or absent. Whatever happens I know that Hardy will be there, and this last quality of comradeship is worshipful: it seems to be the very basic test of manhood. I suppose it is because war makes that test so obviously that its old appeal has force. Courage is a social quality. Out here I see it means caring for your pals more than yourself. For me it has no meaning apart from some degree of friendship.

Fatigues

We are back in the farmhouse at Sailly. Outside in the cobbled courtyard there's a hole in the ground where a shell dropped the other day, killing the captain and two N.C.O.s of the company from whom we took over.

It is something to be out of the trenches for a while, but here, not much; for we provide fatigue-parties every evening to carry materials into the line, and work there most of the night. After a spell of the trenches a succession of nights like this becomes tiring, and my luck has been out, so that I have been on fatigue three nights out of the past four. (By the way, why is work in the army always called "fatigue"?) And here comes the adjutant again.

I protest I have done my share, but he merely condescends to ladle out soft soap about the colonel's good opinion. Well, I'm tired; but there's no saying "No" in this service, so I must rout out my unwilling men as if I enjoyed the job. The devil of it is that they are inclined to esteem an officer in proportion as he is able to dodge these impositions. They must be like him to-night and lump it. The only compensation about doing more than my share is that it lulls the fear of failure. At least I am pulling my oar.

Approaching the guns

We are off to the trenches again, and I declare it will be rest to be there, for I have been in the front line practically every night for the past three weeks.

Getting in and out of the village of Hébuterne has become too adventurous for tired nerves. It looks as if it will be unpleasant again this afternoon, for there's shelling going on in the distance. Now as we begin to cross the plain we see shells dropping near the fresh battery of guns drawn up in line on the western outskirt of the village. Our path runs between the guns, and we are watching the slow traversing of an area we shall very soon have to cross. We have a mile to march, and every step towards that barrier of fire. No wonder our pace seems to drag. If only we could tell where the shell that comes over when we pass will fall!

There's nothing for it but to go on. . . . We are getting to the zone. The shells are falling on our left. But that one was clean on the road! . . . Now we are passing. What's it to be? . . . Our shell falls on the right covering us with dust. We are safe, and would like to put wings to our heels.

A prisoner

Rowley comes back from the front line, where he had been to see Simpkins this morning, with great news. Peeping over the top he saw three Germans quite close to our trenches looking as though they had been out on patrol last night and lost their way. Quickly borrowing a rifle, he covered them. Two of the men ran and escaped, but the third, an officer, who was close under the parapet, put up his hands and came in. Rowley searched him and sent him down the trench to H.Q., keeping his revolver, which he shows me, remarking that he has always wanted one of these automatic revolvers and intends to hang on to this. I fail to see why, for we've no ammunition for it. Still he ought to have a trophy, for it sounds like a fairly smart capture. We do not forget to congratulate him, and he goes up a useful peg in the eyes of the men.

Tear shells

I have just come into the dug-out from wiring. All the while we were at work we heard light shells sailing with a watery whistle high over our heads towards Hébuterne. They flowed on in a stream, and we wondered what they could be, for they burst with very little noise. Now this sickly-sweet pear-drop smell, together with a tingling sensation in the eyes, shows they were what we call tear shells—shells filled with some gas, very harmless in its effects, but sufficiently unpleasant to make the eyes water profusely. They also make uncovered food uneatable and smoking beastly. Those last two effects are particularly offensive to me because my birthday fare, sent from England, lies here in the dug-out wasted, and a hard smoker could do great violence to the man who poisons his tobacco.

This futile waste seems an epitome of the childishness of modern war. The kind of mind that now devises inventions for war would be kept in an imbecile home in any civilised society; such a mind is as far beneath reprobation as contempt.

Gruesome work

Of all ghastly work this digging of a sap through the ground covered in the attack of July 1st is the most horrible. Hill returned from it last night physically sick. There are men buried here four or five feet deep, their bodies often lying as they fell, with the limbs stretched in all directions. We dig among the bodies, and the difficulties that ensue when they lie deep, stretched transversely across the gap, must be imagined, for they will not be described.

Loot

There's trouble brewing over that German officer's revolver. In his examination he said Rowley had taken it from him, and on the same day a "chit" comes down from the colonel asking Rowley to hand it over. He replies that he hasn't got it. Another chit comes along to say search must be made for it and the revolver handed in at once. Rowley duly orders a search to be made —with the natural result. That doesn't satisfy the colonel, who seems to have his suspicions. Meantime Rowley, who has made elaborate arrangements for smuggling the precious weapon home, is not feeling very happy about it. His store of fairy-tales is getting exhausted. I wonder whether the storm will stay in the tea-cup.

Devilment?

Hardy reports that the colonel went round the front line this afternoon, and, not content with that, insisted on wandering about on top and compelling a reluctant subaltern to follow him. Opinion is divided upon whether the colonel was sober. It is not disputed that he starts the day with whisky and drinks late into the night, but the defence declares he is never drunk and is a

man without fear. I am only convinced that
whisky is an unmitigated curse in wartime. Men
take to it in time of strain: the strain is unre-
lieved; then what are they to do? The distillers
should be great patriots. I believe they are.

The patrol

It has been raining sharply, but now at ten
o'clock the sky clears and the full moon makes
dark the shadows of the trenches. I meet Rowley
with a chit in his hand, which he reads by the
moonlight. He is to send out one officer and ten
men who will bring in a German prisoner, dead
or alive, for purposes of identification. "And I'm
afraid," he adds apologetically, "it's your turn."

The time, the moonlight and the siting of the
trenches make this order as nearly impossible as
the improbable can be. Rowley agrees. It ought
to have been tried when the sky was dark and
before patrols went in. Thinking it probable that
the colonel sent the order before the sky cleared,
I ask Rowley if he will have it confirmed. No.
Orders are orders, even when they come in the
form of plain invitations to suicide. I'd better
go out and make a show, and together we'll cook
the report. Here's a vile quandary. Is the colonel
aware that the battalion intelligence officer went
out with a sergeant and a couple of men two
hours ago and has not yet returned? Besides,

with ten men, across one hundred yards of no-
man's land, on a night when you can see from
wire to wire! A first-class cut-throat might stand
a chance, working alone; but even he would avoid
such a night.

The mere receipt of such an order seems like
an insult. I shall not attempt to carry it out, and
that not only for my own sake; but I should like
to see the colonel and be clear with him. That's
impossible.

Sick at heart and savage in temper, I pick my
men and lead them down a disused forward sap.
Well away from our own trenches, it becomes
uncanny work creeping along in the shadows,
stick in one hand, revolver in the other, not knowing what we may confront round the next bend,
I turn to see the men and find the corporal,
who bragged so much about his skill at such ex-
ploits, holding back at a very safe distance. We
go on. Then suddenly, out from our left, there
comes a long whistle. A moment later it is replied
to by a similar signal on our right. We wait and
then go on again. The signal is repeated. That
is enough for me. I reckon we are seen and tell
the men to get back.

Down in the dug-out Rowley and I write a report that is as near lying as can be without being
actual falsehood. The whole business makes me
angry. I suppose I am wanting in humour.

Missing

I hear the colonel was not pleased with the report. I also hear that the other party started off from the same point, and that they still have not returned. It is presumed they are captured, as they well might have been when the sky suddenly cleared. Captured or dead, the colonel is said to be vexed with them. I wonder what would have happened had we gone on? My resentment at being sent on such a fool's errand is not allayed by this news.

Chits about the German officer's revolver have stopped at last. Rowley is relieved.

Farewell to Hébuterne

This starry night is our last at Hébuterne. At midnight we are marching to Bayencourt, and Rowley says we are going right out on rest. It is so bright a prospect one is tempted to entertain it as a certainty; but hope mustn't rise too high while we are still in trenches; expectation must remain in the shadow a few hours longer, knowing that not an hour, ten minutes, or even a single moment, is yet within the bounds of common certainty. Still, with ordinary luck . . .

Either they've decided that the support trenches are too far back, or they want reserve trenches for "kicking-off" in an attack that's impending. We are out on top between the first and second lines, and have begun digging. It is wonderfully quiet.

If the Germans only knew, they could make it hot for us; but by some extraordinary coincidence they have even stopped their machine-guns to-night. This is all the more remarkable because of the distinct change that has come over the place since that summer afternoon, ages ago, when we first took over.

'Tisn't bad now, but it can be no longer called a quiet front; and those batteries outside the village seem to augur trouble to come. With any luck we shall be out of that, stretching our limbs for a while in the realms of civilisation—seeing shops and inhabited houses and the faces of well-dressed women—aware, by contact with it, that there is another world in being beside this place of fear and devastation. In the first large town we stay at I shall go to the best *pâtisserie* in the place and order *café-au-lait* and a dozen *éclairs*. Hill and I will eat them sitting on steady chairs, wearing clean clothes, in a room so fresh and bright we could eat off the floor. Then we shall . . .

Wait a while! We are not out yet.

How well these miners dig! We could give points to the Guards and beat them at digging.

It is midnight. We begin to pack up. Still the quiet continues. This is a gift from the gods. Down through the trenches, under the trees. Hullo! They are not going to let us go without a salute. Scissz! Plonk! They are wide of the mark. We are leaving them behind. Good-bye, you damned old trenches! May you all be covered in before we see you again. Not a man of my platoon does this evil ground cover. Come on, my merry men; but not too fast for self-respect. Another "bit" of the Great War's over. Here's level ground again. Another mile or two and you will sing, if you're not too sleepy.

Going westward

It is cheering to be going westward: the farther you go in this direction the more human the world becomes. Roads in repair, trees, houses, civilians at their civil tasks, old women whitening their doorsteps, old men threshing corn—all the un-marshalled ease of common life appears again. It is welcome to our eyes as light to the blind, for every common object of civilisation looks like a work of art. I actually fell in love with a lamp-post at Doullens.

Billets at Halloy

Here we are at Halloy again, but the days (or rather nights) of sleeping in thin canvas shelters are over. We woke last night to find the rain pouring through, making the uneven ground a series of pools. The men of course fared worse, and we have had to find fresh billets all round. I am ashamed to see the men in the hovel they've got. In England a tramp wouldn't sleep in it; but the town-major declares nothing else is to be had at

the moment, and we are moving on to-morrow.
We officers of C Company have obtained reluctant
permission from the farm which adjoins the
orchard to sleep in a stable. At least it's dry and
has a loft for the orderlies overhead; but we are
none too pleased with our host for his unwilling-
ness to give us the shelter accorded to beasts. The
orderlies repeat the old tale about having to pay
for a glass of water.

Grilled chicken

The army canteen was low in supplies yesterday
and army rations will never move a gourmet to
eloquence; nevertheless we have just fed like
princes. We have tasted the sweets—or rather the
entrées—of adversity; for if it hadn't been for
the adversity of our host, well, we might have
managed the sweets, but the entrée would have
been as Castlereagh says—"Napoo." When hungry men are sick of bully beef, barndoor fowls
should remain in barns. They ought to be warned
against strutting between a hungry man's legs.
Sikes, Smalley's servant, first noticed them. He
would. Rumour says he's a professional burglar in
civil life. That is no doubt flattery; but Sikes certainly knows something of the fine art of poaching.
After whispering between him and Smalley, and
sundry nods and smiles between them and Rowley,
certain assignations were approved whereby our
prospects brightened, and happy in hope we re-

tired to rest—all except Sikes and Castlereagh, who appeared coming down from the loft with a sack. We waited and listened; but not a sound was heard, not a funeral cluck. Then back to the loft they bore them.

We had grilled chicken for lunch to-day, and I defy Sherlock Holmes to find a feather.

Out on rest

Halloy to Barly—Barly to Maizicourt—Maizicourt to Caours: that has been our itinerary for the past three days' marching. Once we are on the march, things are pretty much the same. We go right into the country, billet at a village farm, where the men sleep in the barns and the officers take whatever accommodation the farmhouse will give. This of course varies. Barly was clean, Maizicourt dirty—and no wonder considering that midden. We slept eight in one small room at Maizicourt. Still, any billet is lavender after a day's march, even if it doesn't smell quite like it.

We wander on, passing from place to place, never arriving, till one has the sensation of moving in a trance. As a child I remember being worried over a kaleidoscope, because I could never determine the one pattern which really *was* the kaleidoscope. Now here the same desire to shake the frame of things till they fall into settled reality comes over me. But we go on, moved like pawns in a game of chess, by minds that do not declare their intentions, to fates which even the players do not know.

Now we are at Caours and rumour says we are staying for sixteen days. Abbeville is only three miles away, and just to walk into a town outside a marching column and have a bath and a meal served will be luxury and adventure. Here, too, we can get through some much-needed training with those new drafts that have recently been dribbling into the regiment.

This is a fairly large village—suburb perhaps it should be called—yet we had difficulty in finding billets. The French people are not hospitable to English troops, and naturally there's a good deal of soreness on that score. Yet I can see the picture from their angle. English soldiers are not the finest exponents of delicate manners. Dourness and hoggishness easily appear after a spell in the trenches, and to the lips of gay-mannered folk like the French I've no doubt the adjective *bête* rises easily when they are asked suddenly to open their rooms to rough, dirty-looking herds. You have to be very charitable before you open your house gladly to officers who are a little lousy, usually none too well-bred, and sometimes quite anxious to seduce your servants. Anyway, we are not the guests in French houses we were in English billets.

The rooms of this big country house are nearly all shut up: the owner is away in Paris; but we can only have the use of two bedrooms *via* the back staircase, and these only because French law

obliges the owner to give us that amount of accommodation. We have to pay three francs a day
for permission to mess at an estaminet half a
mile from the billet. We needed all our philosophy,
after a long, hot march to look upon this great
empty place with its walled garden and big
kitchens, and then learn that our orderlies must
make a camp-fire in a neighbouring field before we
could have a cup of tea, and that our sanitary
squad must provide for our other physical needs
by digging.

Well, there 'tis; with this moral. No civil popu-
lation can endure a military one for long.

Abbeville

Hill has been sent on a Lewis-gun course at le
Touquet, so my jaunt to Abbeville is with Hardy
and Smalley. In the town we meet Jenkins, a new
subaltern who has just been attached to our company, and after a bath we have dinner together
at a hotel that is crowded with officers. 'Tis strange
to be treading pavement and looking in shop-
windows again: so reminiscent that it tugs at the
heart, and in a second one is wondering why one
wanders here so idly when across only a few miles
of water lives another—perhaps at this very hour
wandering in London—whose living presence is
all one lives for: whose living form one may never
see again. To banish the thought we buy trinkets
and trifles, and then go to the beautiful Gothic
church. What centuries of deep religious purpose-

ful life raised these arching pillars and made this form and beauty! How deeply it impresses, though the spirit that animated the life of those people is fled! How those history-books of successive wars traduced the life of the past! Places like this were not built by hands that knew war as we know it. We and our khaki are out of our element. Let's get away. Besides, there is little inducement to stop; for a service is on, and from the pulpit a villainous-faced priest is repeating a litany in Latin that must remain unintelligible to all but initiates, since it sounds like nothing but a rapid and nasal repetition of the words *"Daily Mail."* Spoken by other lips, in other tones, in other times, who knows but this very litany was a thing of awe and beauty. Why seek we the living among the dead? The spirit of the old religion is now to be found in its churches only when they are empty.

What now? Shall we go back? Jenkins scoffs at the idea. He is a fat, comical figure, oddly possessed of a very nimble brain. He has no intention of going back without enjoying some sort of feminine society. Ah me! And what wouldn't I give for my sort! But any sort? And that hired? I try to persuade them good-humouredly to return with me. They smile too knowingly; so I jog back alone.

There are other pities in the world beside this war, and of all I know, this war-begotten waste of feeling now looks heaviest.

OCTOBER

OCTOBER

"The offensive spirit"

$\mathcal{M}$Y NEW SERGEANT HAS TAKEN
over. He is a dapper, intelligent little fellow
—rather young to be a sergeant, but a welcome
change from that lazy old ruffian. I would have
preferred to remain with the company just now;
but courses seem the order of the day. Not only
Hill is gone; Smalley is on a bombing course,
Hardy attached to some sort of tunnelling sec-
tion, and I have begun a bayonet course.

I wonder how Hamlet would have fared with
a bayonet? He must have been no bad hand at
rapiers.

The course is laid out at a field two miles away,
and there we cultivate ferocity before sacks once
again, and learn most ungentlemanly ways of dis-
patching our enemies. From the standpoint of
realism a good deal is wanting, and as the week
goes by the sergeant-major in charge of the course
has difficulty in preventing our exercises from be-
coming a mere sporting competition as gaily undertaken as a rugger match. We are inclined to go
over the track too much like children playing at
Indians in search of scalps. I am convinced the

proper spirit of animosity cannot be inculcated by such methods. They are too direct. Any newspaper editor could teach the army more excellent ways. The army seems dimly aware of this. It does its best, though very clumsily I think.

Yesterday the whole battalion marched out to a quarry not far from here and, in the natural amphitheatre, heard a lecture by a Scottish officer on "The Spirit of the Bayonet."

From a purely military standpoint it was excellent. Why, indeed, should we spare a fat German just because he throws up his hands and shouts "Kamarad," when, as the lecturer says, if we let him live, he may become the father of ten more Huns? Killing is the job for infantrymen, and if we don't like killing, why did we join the infantry? The bayonet is the logical conclusion of all fighting: there you get to the real thing; and a proper lust for blood is what you need to use a bayonet. What sapient fool thinks he's going to do his country credit without it? But we mustn't overdo it. Three inches is enough. Don't go and bury the muzzle of your rifle in your man and then find you can't get your bayonet out, no matter how hard you stamp on him. "In," "out," and then ready for the next, is the way.

Yes, I've no doubt this kind of instruction is quite necessary, and it is futile to start wondering upon what terms this bloodthirsty incarnation of hate lives with his wife. As has been said, "There's a war on." But I cannot help wishing all the parsonry, who so kindly praise our noble Christian sacrifice, could have a little of this tonic. They might then, with the Bishop of London in command, be sent on a bayonet charge. "The stern reality" looks so different when you make a trade of wrapping it in a phrase.

The effect of the lecture was probably different upon different hearers. For my part, I confess to a weak stomach.

Tanks

We are still out "on rest," but it isn't quite so restful as it sounds. Last night, 8 to 11:30:—a night march on a compass bearing. To-day, 6.30 to 8:—adjutant's parade. 9.30 to 10.30:—close-order drill. 10.30 to 11:—walk out to brigade bayonet course. 11 to 2.30:—bayonet fighting and returning. 3.30 to 5:—assistant officer at pay of company. 7.30 to 9.30:—walk to Brigade H.Q. for lecture on Tanks and back again.

The lecture on Tanks was a little disappointing. We were all agog to hear about these new land-caterpillars that, according to the papers, have done such marvellous things in the recent push on the Somme, knocking down houses and trees, careering over trenches and frightening the Germans out of their wits. But the Tanks' officer put rather a damper on our hopes.

He started off by pooh-poohing the newspaper

reports as exaggerations of the patriotic imagination, and explained that tanks have to go very carefully, or they get stuck in T-places where communication-trenches join the line. He also said they were quite vulnerable underneath and on top, and instead of painting the glowing picture of infantrymen marching in their wake triumphantly to Berlin, he cynically told us our chief duty in regard to the tanks would be to provide a squad to march in front of them and drag the wounded out of the way: a none too healthy job, he added, as of course a tank draws the enemy fire. Finally he reminded us that of course tanks were too heavy to use on very soft ground, and, with the winter coming on, their general employment would probably be delayed till the spring.

Now rain is falling heavily again, and the weather seems to have broken up. Thank God we're not in the line yet, though we are moving soon. I wish people who talk cheerfully about the campaigns of next spring would lecture only to the folks at home. A day at a time is enough for us out here.

"Fed up"

We are on the march again, now going east. It rained heavily almost every day of our last week at Caours. The winter has begun.

Last night we slept at Conteville: now we are at Frohen-le-Grand, and again it is raining. I suppose I am depressed by the weather, but quite possibly by the fact that we are on our way to that place of desolation again. I wonder how, in God's name, we do go on with this life! Looked at from an individual standpoint it is the very insanity of slavery. This endless hideous life of the automaton —I shall never get used to it. I am too old. Perhaps if I were seventeen I shouldn't mind. I should know so little that was different, and this would only seem a perpetual, rather unpleasant boarding-school. I should have less memory and be less inclined to reflect. I shouldn't be carrying about a heart that's fixed: it might easily be the bladder on a fool's stick. But now sometimes the thought that I may never again know any other life than this affects me like a madness. My God! I understand desertion. A man distraught determines that the last act of his life shall at least be one of his own volition; and who can say that what is commonly regarded as the limit of cowardice is not then heroic?

But the job out here's not done. The Germans are still in France. While that is so, who can talk of peace? Truly there's nothing I'd sooner be doing than helping to push the Germans out of France. Why can't the devils go of their own accord? It would settle everything. If they only retired to their own frontier, for my part the war would be over tomorrow. But they don't; so all the loathsomeness of this life is swallowed up in the consideration that the work is fundamentally good to anyone who is fit for it. I am fit. I shall go on, even gladly. But it is hell.

The new Captain

Our old Don Juan, Rowley, is on Paris leave, which has been instituted because the U-boats have weakened the Channel service and stopped home leave for the time. In his place we have Captain Lancy, who has been out in France a long time, though he has not seen the trenches recently, being lucky enough to hold a town-majorship for a good-ish while. We shall be glad when Rowley comes back, for Lancy is snivelling and pernickety. Having no natural authority, he adopts a disagreeable air as a substitute, and while he is competent enough from the orderly-room standpoint, the men dislike him: when the nondescript of weak character poses as the strong man of discipline they are not deceived.

Hardy and Hill are back, and now we meet Lancy at the billet to receive news which is to be given us in great secrecy. Lancy can hardly bring himself to deliver it, so great is his sense of importance while he holds information we lack.

After pledging our silence he begins:

"There's going to be an attack at Hébuterne very shortly, and you fellows are going over with the company. Number nine platoon will take the German front line, 'Fall.' Number ten will go on and take the support trench, 'Fame.' Number eleven will go over both those lines and take 'Fate.' Smalley as our company bomber will clear the communication-trenches and help you to consolidate when he comes up. That's the bare outline. Of course you'll get details, but we're going to practise this stunt on ground marked out at Halloy; so the C.O. thought it as well that you fellows should know what you are practising for. You're not to tell the men anything—not even the N.C.O.s."

"And where will you be?" I inquire.

Lancy smiles with satisfaction.

"I shall be in our front line to receive messages; and, by the way, don't forget: you send a runner back as soon as ever you've taken the trench. I shall want to know at once."

Nothing more is said; but his obvious pleasure at taking a back seat in this stunt does not raise him in our esteem. As to the "show" itself, only Hardy is pleased with the prospect. He declares he is sick of "arsing about the trenches waiting to get pipped. Now there'll be a chance of a good 'blighty.' Death or glory, and a good job too. If you're killed that finishes it."

I remember that German wire and wonder what sort of bombardment can ever cut it enough to

give us a chance; for their wire is not like ours;
it is heavily stranded and has barbs about an inch
long.

In any case an attack is bound to be a foul business. In the way of personal fighting, I devoutly
hope I shan't be too hideously involved.

Back to Halloy

A day of sun and cool wind, perfect for marching, and the luck to be at the head of the column,
immediately behind our newly formed drum-and-
fife band, made the march to Halloy a pleasure.
The noble band is only eight flutes, six bugles and
six drums; but a little band goes a long way to
shorten the road: even its failures, greeted with
cheering, help men to keep their eyes off the
"Boots-boots-boots-boots movin' up and down
again!" They've a rotten billet here again: a
tumbledown old barn, with no straw in it, and a
stinking midden just outside. I've had the midden
cleared and given them inner relief for external
discomfort. Tins of fish, tinned apricots, five hundred cigarettes and some sweets. Lord! what a
mixture; but it was all that could be had at the
engineers' canteen.

We are back in our barn, and whatever is
thought, nothing is said about those fowls lately
deceased.

Practising the attack

We have been at Halloy a week, drilling, training and practising our stunt. First we did it by spoken orders in daylight: then by the watch: then by spoken orders at night: finally by the watch at night. Out here, where there are no shells dropping about, where we have to imagine our own barrage-fire and all the enemy elects to put up in reply, we can do it perfectly, and a pretty tame affair it looks. It would be howled out of the arena at a military tournament. No dashing, hell-for-leather, with wide throats and bayonets extended: just men getting up for no apparent reason and going forward at a slow marching-pace in extended order for a given distance, followed by others doing precisely the same, time and distance being almost everything. Over and over again we have impressed upon us the necessity of keeping close up to the barrage: even if we have a few casualties from our own fire, we are told that our only chance lies in keeping close up.

Hardy is getting dead keen, and with Hill and Smalley coming too, one couldn't be better accompanied; but what lies at the back of my mind all the time is the recollection of that German wire. I believe they might shell it for weeks and still we should get hung up.

Odd, and yet not so odd, the weeding out that's already gone on among the little crowd that left Charing Cross with me three months ago. Brun-

ning and Leonard are both back with rheumatism.
Zenu had the bad luck to break his leg practising
bayonet-fighting. Another one of them has gone
into a venereal hospital. Altogether Hill and I are
the only two left. Poor Jenkins! It will be some
time before he sees fighting. The morning he returned from Abbeville he told me he had spent the
night with "a perfect artist." Now he too is in the
venereal hospital.

The dream and the business

I haven't *solved* the Front. By that I mean
imagination and actuality are not yet at one; and
in handling any problem it seems to me you haven't
the whip-hand of it until imagination and actuality
are at one. Whenever I see the Front in the light
of what made me join the army—whenever I think
of the whole business as a task, then I welcome the
Front and feel I can eat fire easily. Imaginatively
I have it all right. But when I shrink to little
actuality and think of watery trenches, sinister-
looking crump-holes, barbed wire, machine-guns,
bombs, and most of all big guns and intensive shelling, then the whole place becomes a land of foreboding, even of horror, where blind Death keeps
groping hideously. It becomes a place I would give
anything to keep out of, as you would a house that
threatened every minute to fall about your ears.

But these two images have to become one before
you have solved the Front, and in my case I know

that can only come about when actuality has been wholly swallowed up by imagination. Then there will be unity, and I shall no longer be perpetually passing from one extreme state of mind to the other.

Somehow I must get hold of a sense of true proportion and be able to keep it, and not let the first law of Nature, or any other individual consideration, play old Harry by setting up a dualism which destroys the dream in the misery of the business.

When I can do that I shall have solved the Front. It is like focussing the lenses of these field-glasses. There is a spot where you get perfect sight with both eyes; but it takes finding.

Cinema films

I've just come across a bundle of old newspapers giving accounts of the film of the Somme battle now being shown at the Scala in London. Those "cheery columns of men going into action" were unwittingly a little deceptive, I fancy. Not that I would say a word disparaging the men, Heaven knows. But, in the first place that comfortably seated audience should be told that a camera out here is a phenomenon and a reminder of home which any men anywhere would greet with cheers. And, in the second, I should like to insist that men going into action are usually frightfully depressed at first, so that they grouse, curse their luck, and then become silent and brooding. Later, just to keep their courage up, and because they feel something has to be done, they start singing "Pack up your troubles in your old kit-bag," get excited, and feel their troubles *are* over—until a shell bursts near. Then the silence is grim. Here and there a fatalist is gay because he believes he is "booked for a blighty"; but men are not such fools as to be glad to be going into the hell of attack.

The cinema can show some things, but, great Heavens! what a gap lies between looking *at* war on a screen and being *in* it.

War history

There's another cutting from these newspapers here which is amusing to me. It also goes to show how hard it will be for anyone to write the true history of this war.

The report says that on one of the nights when we happened to be in the line at St. George's Hill, the Germans were seen leaving their trenches, but were driven back by the Allied barrage-fire before they could reach our line.

Now the true history of that little episode is this. There were strict orders at the time that S.O.S. signals were only to be used in extreme emergency. A certain company-commander (close to us, but not of our battalion) became unnecessarily alarmed and sent up his S.O.S. rockets. The concentrated fire was given, and the Germans, apparently thinking we were going to attack, replied in kind just in front of the British trenches. Absolutely nothing else happened. On neither side did the men attempt to leave their trenches. But the company-commander had to save his face. Hence the report; received no doubt with enormous armchair satisfaction. Probably the German version was precisely similar.

Changed plans

The attack at Hébuterne is cancelled; no one knows why. The colonel has gone on leave, and to-morrow we march south. It looks as if we were bound for the Somme again. The only one who is not pleased with the news is Hardy. He is genuinely disappointed. "Now we shall be here for the whole bloody winter," he remarks.

I wonder.

Beauquesne

We are at Talmas, a village lying midway between Doullens and Amiens. After heavy rain last night it has been a delicious day, and the landscape between Beauquesne and Talmas, wooded and hilly, looked entrancing in the still, clear, autumn air. I had a fine opportunity to enjoy it, for I was orderly-officer for the day, which meant that I came on two hours after the battalion, bringing with me the twenty men who were left behind to clear up the billets. At Beauquesne we passed some large country houses that are said to be in use as army headquarters. One could not help admiring the command's taste.

Méaulte

For the past three days we have marched about ten miles a day. Last night we halted at Franvillers: to-day we found ourselves back on the old road, passing our hillside at Dernancourt: now we are billeted in Méaulte. I hate this place. It lies low, near the Ancre, and has the dejected utilitarian air of a poor industrial town. It is one of those waste places that are neither in nor out of the line. Shells still come over occasionally, as if to show their contempt and complete the dilapidation. Méaulte has a hang-dog look. Almost every house is used by troops for one purpose or another, and all the country round it is strewn with dumps and the refuse of the army scrap-heap. On its churned-up roads, over which the stream of traffic never ceases to pass, pitifully miserable-looking German prisoners work, scraping and sweeping. In their dirty ragged clothing they look more woebegone than the inhabitants of any slum. They are passed by like dogs by everyone.

Our billet is as cheerless. It is a matchboarded upper room without door or fireplace. Its dirty floor and scribbled walls appear to have been used by troops since the beginning of the war, and of course there is not a stick of furniture in the room.

Down below is a dirty little grocer's shop. A woman actually keeps it on. Why she is allowed to remain I cannot think. Rowley, who is just back, no sooner heard of her than he vowed he would make her close acquaintance.

To crown all, the rain drizzles down.

The concert

We have now had three days of rain in this place. Rowley decided yesterday that something must be done to cheer the fellows up; so we had an impromptu concert in a large outhouse, big enough to hold most of the men. As a concert it was not a success. We had no piano, and our stock of choruses soon ran out. Before the evening was half over, every officer, and then every humorist of the company, had taken his turn at speech-making, and finally we fell back upon the inevitable improper story. Even that didn't raise much merriment. Impropriety should be served as a savoury: it needs the background of polite society to give it relish; but we had no background, so the sharp contrast which makes humour was lacking, and we were forced back on grossness, which is dull. Still, we had beer, a full barrel of it, and all the cigarettes we could lay hands on; and certainly we wished each other well. I suppose I am a rank idealist, but Lord! how far this was from what one would wish to give these men.

The sentence

We parade to hear the sentence of court-martial on a boy who has been found guilty of refusing to obey the order of a corporal. Between the armed guards stands the prisoner, bareheaded, without rifle or belt. The sentence is forty-one days' Field Punishment No. 1. The boy receives his helmet and belt and returns to the ranks. He will begin to expiate his crime— (if he is still alive) when we next come out of the trenches.

The story behind this little drama is as follows. The corporal has been recently promoted. He and the boy were pals in the ranks. They failed to adjust the old relationship to the new conditions, and the corporal, being proud of his dignity, asserted his authority rather heavily. Finally the army, if appealed to, has to maintain the authority of its officers. But forty-one days' No. 1!

Well, the army only pretends to rough justice. Sometimes it seems very rough.

To end war?

"A war to end war." I used to wonder whether it wasn't possible: whether by demonstrating the impossibility of reaching a decisive issue, this war would not convince the nations of the futility of war. To-day I came across this:

> *But vain the sword and vain the bow*
> *They never can work war's overthrow.*

I see it is absolutely true. No policeman ever yet improved the world's morals. There's no hope from negation. War is like the rash of a disease —bound to come out if the body politic is not healthy. The patient pities himself when the fever is on him; but not by self-pity nor antagonism to disease will he escape infection.

There were two more lines to the quatrain:

> *The hermit's prayer and the widow's tear*
> *Alone can free the world from fear.*

What does that mean? "The hermit's prayer" I think must mean thought energised: thought that is more than thinking. And "the widow's tear" I take to be an image of the deepest pity of love.

Deeper thought and deeper pity. They are both beyond the sentimentality and hard-faced government between which weakness alternates.

One cannot imagine a future for the kind of government that makes its final arbitrament the placing of vast numbers of men in an area of flying iron. Common-sense repudiates that. That is not government, even by force.

Is there any other way of raising the ethical standard of government other than by the example of individuals? I suppose that was Tolstoy's idea. Conscientious objection to war seems a blind alley; but then every affirmation implies a negative. To contemporaries the Crucifixion must have looked an utter negation.

A tent in the mud

Another move forward. We are now in tents at Mansel Copse, which lies between Mametz and Carnoy. When we arrived, just before midday, the troops we were relieving still occupied the tents. We therefore waited an hour or so on the hillside opposite. The road below us was no-man's land on July 1st, and again we looked over the desolation of the old battlefield. Under a grey sky the place was hardly recognisable as that which Hardy and I first saw on that hot morning in August. The desolation now appeared even greater, though the whole area was as active as an ant-heap.

When they did go, the outgoing troops were too hurried to clear up their own refuse; and what with the mud and their muck, friction occurred between our companies over the disposal of the tents. Rowley, who is not given to complaining, was rather badly aggrieved to find C Company short of room. Even with sufficient room, tents on the bare soaking clay, at this time of year, would not be very desirable places.

However, we have made shift. As far as the officers are concerned there are five of us in a bell-tent, with heaps of boots, clothes, books and food piled up on our valises, until we do indeed look like an expeditionary force. Judged by appearances we might be bound for the North Pole. It is very cold, so we have rigged up a stove in the centre of the tent. This stove is a marvellous contrivance.

It consists of an old petrol-tin for base: a big piece of pipe with holes knocked in it for a brazier, surmounted by a damaged steel helmet; and finally on top of that a bit of stove-pipe to serve for a chimney. This juts from a hole in the helmet out of the tent-door. Not all the smoke can be persuaded to leave the tent by the chimney; but though we occasionally weep and choke, we are warm.

The doctor drops into the mêlée. He is a genial young to middle-aged man. We rag him; but, after endangering his life by knocking him into the stove, make room and welcome his yarns.

"Feather beds"

All officers are required by the colonel, who returned in time to bring the battalion out of Méaulte. Never having been wanted by the C.O. in a body except for a "strafe," there is much speculation as to what can be the matter now. We bundle out of the tent into the mud, and plough our way to the small marquee that adjoins the orderly-room tent.

It is at once evident that the colonel is under a misapprehension. He understands officers made a general complaint about their own quarters this morning. Of course they did nothing of the kind. The feud, such as it was, had been simply an inter-company matter over the question of disposal. He makes his mistake unpleasantly clear, and we hear his comments with as good grace as possible, till he remarks ferociously that, if we think we have come to France for nothing but feather-beds and women, he will damn well show us we haven't.

I don't know how this vulgarity affects the others, but it fills me with a desire to plant my fist in his face; and this for more reasons than the fact that I have not had a bed since I landed. The jibe comes from the wrong quarter. While I hear him talking sullenly about the shell-holes we are going to occupy up the line to-morrow, I find myself wondering, all the time, whether the choice of regular officers to command line battalions is confined to gentlemen of this quality.

No: it is sheer bad luck; for I call to mind the colonel of another regiment in our brigade, a rather elderly officer who walked over to the German trenches on July 2nd, accompanied only by his orderly, just to prove (what was not believed) that the trenches were empty—and I see a kindly, sober, humorous English gentleman.

A piteous appeal

Rowley has received a pitiable letter, signed by two or three influential people in a Northern town, setting forth the case of a mother nearly demented because she has had two of her three sons killed in the trenches since July 1st, and is in mortal fear of what may happen to the sole surviving member of the family, a boy in our company named Stream. They are petitioning the Prime Minister for his release to less dangerous duty, and meantime ask if we can do anything.

Rowley is helpless at the moment, but he has shown the letter to the colonel, who promises to see what can be done next time we are out.

A bad start

We are on the road to Montauban in the grey morning following a wet night. We can only march very slowly, with frequent halts, for traffic blocks the way and the road is being covered with loose granite. Returning troops face us, and we have to "form two-deep" to let them go by.

Good Lord! That captain's face was a sight! Grey-green, like the cheeks of the dead, and his eyes fixed and staring. The men following him are smothered in mud. They are hardly by when a boy in my platoon, newly arrived with one of the fresh drafts, falls down in a fit. I get my cane between his teeth and, as he lies foaming on the ground, wonder how this child of the factories, an obvious epileptic, can have slipped through the doctor's fingers. He soon comes round and is returned to the nearest dressing-station. On we go. It is an unpropitious start.

The Major shines

The battalion is halted at midday on sloping ground above Trônes Wood, waiting while the cooks at the field-kitchens do their best, in the drizzling rain, to make us a hot stew. The colonel has gone on with company-commanders to take over at the trenches. On this slope there are a number of tarpaulins stretched tentwise over the ground to provide low shelters, and into these the men scramble out of the wet. Each one is overcrowded by half a dozen men. Others go down to explore the dug-outs in the wood below, and then return to recount horrors to be seen in that gruesome place. 'Tis bad enough here when someone's heel catches a lump in the ground and reveals a man's putrefying arm.

The cooks signal that they are ready, and the men troop across the field with their mess-tins. The company has not been handed over to me, and I am unaware that I am in charge of it; but while the men are returning word comes that I am required by Major Smythe. I see him on the other side of the field: march across and salute. He wants to know what the hell I mean by allowing men to go for their meal in that manner, and pauses imposingly for an answer. I have been soldiering long enough to know one does not answer the rhetorical questions of superior officers, more especially when the officer happens to be a figurehead. So I take my cursing in silence, half amused to note the change that has come over the very amiable and hurried gentleman I once pursued round the bays at Hébuterne. But I reflect, as I return, what an incorrigibly unsoldierly **unit I**

must be; for even had I known I was in command,
it would never have occurred to me that the men
needed marching.

Desolation on the Somme

In the dusk of a leaden afternoon we march
away from Trônes Wood through Guillemont and
Ginchy. On the eastern side of the tiny village of
Ginchy we are suddenly confronted with a wide,
rolling, open plain over which there is no road
but only a single "duck-walk" track. Slowly the
battalion stretches itself out in single file along
this track, and one by one the men follow each
other, till the trail extends like the vertebræ of
an endless snake. On either side lies the open plain.
Not a sign of life is anywhere to be seen, but instead there appear, in countless succession, stretching as far as the eye can pierce the gloom, shell-
holes filled with water. The sense of desolation
these innumerable, silent, circular pools produce
is horrible, so vividly do they remind me of a
certain illustration by Doré to Dante's *Inferno,*
that I begin to wonder whether I have not stepped
out of life and entered one of the circles of the
damned; and as I look upon these evil pools I half
expect to see a head appearing from each one.
Here and there the succession of pools is broken
by what appear in the fading light to be deep
yawning graves, and over these our duck-walk
makes a frail and slippery bridge.

On and on we go. Jog, jog, jog behind one another, till slowly the merciful darkness shuts out
all sight of this awful land of foreboding. But now
the difficulty of our march increases, for many of
the laths of these duck-boards are broken, and in
the darkness a man trips and falls, pitching his
sand-bag of rations or box of bombs into the mud
that lies deep on either side of the track. Whenever this happens, the rest of the battalion behind
him has to halt while he picks himself up, recovers
his load and steadies himself on the track again
before trying to make good the gap between himself and the man in front. Despite the cautions
passed along the file a hundred times: "Look out"
—"Mind the gap"—"Hole there," these mishaps
constantly occur, till we in the rear wonder why
in the name of Heaven long halts should be needed
when those in front must still be miles from the
trenches. At last the men in front move, and on
we go again. On and on, till it seems we must be
seeking the very end of nowhere, for still the Verey
lights, which will show us the line of the trenches,
do not appear. Every now and then shells drop,
sometimes near enough to spatter us with mud and
make us shudder to think what kind of death we
should meet if one dropped near enough to lift us
into the watery, muddy depths of a shell-hole. But
even the shells seem to be wandering, for they
come fitfully, as if they were fired from nowhere
and had lost their way.

On and on we go. It is getting towards midnight now. The duck-walk ceases and we come out on high grass-land, where the going is good so long as we keep to the crest of the hill and pick a careful way between the shell-holes. Now we are turning and gently descending the hill. The waspish flight of whiz-bangs is heard quite close. We must be near the line at last, though it is still out of sight. Now we drop into mud ankle-deep. A man shouts it is up to the knees where he stands. New voices are heard. The company is no longer extended. There is Rowley. We have arrived.

Across twenty yards of quagmire rough trenches are dimly visible. They are the reserve trenches—ours. The men clamber into them and wrap themselves in their ground-sheets. We have reached the mud.

The little dug-out

"Cheerio, Rowley! This is all right."

"Yes, bloody awful, isn't it? You've got the rations?"

"Yes. Do you know how long we're here for?

"Two days, they said; but I expect it'll be four. Come down the dug-out if you can find room. I must see this fellow off. Lilley's down there and Collins. Collins 'll have to turf out. We've got no room for damned Lewis-gunners."

I follow him down a dozen steep slippery steps; water runs down them, but in spite of this Collins

is sitting on the bottom step. The air below is hot
and thick: the dug-out is not more than six feet
square, and there are now six of us. The captain
of the company we are relieving accepts another
drink, and wishing us luck climbs out. We take off
our equipment, but the quarters are too close for
anything like comfort. Lilley sits on a case of
German soda-water which he opens and finds is
full.

Fancy Lilley being in such a place! The sight
of him brings home and beauty to mind, and we
are soon talking about both. Lilley, it appears,
was married on his last leave, so the conversation
veers round to the institution of marriage. Rowley
thinks it a failure, Lilley a dream. My view is
summed up in the wish that my wife were here.

There is little to be done outside, so we talk the
night away and discuss civilisation as if it still
existed for us, dozing between whiles, eating
raisins, drinking whisky and taking the air when
the fug becomes unbearable.

Near Lesbœufs

Here, by daylight, outside the dug-out, there is
nothing within sight to give an inkling of where
we are. The front line is said to be over the crest
of the sloping ground on our right, about a thousand yards from this spot, but nothing of it is
to be seen, and on all sides nothing but open rolling

downs. A map is the only guide, and that instructs us we are between Gueudecourt and Lesbœufs, rather nearer Lesbœufs than Gueudecourt, though both villages are out of sight. The map declares a windmill once stood here. There is not a trace of it now. Facing the line, H.Q. dug-out is forward on our left, hidden in a sunken road, and the second line runs somewhere just beyond it. The trenches our men occupy are negligible hastily-thrown-up dykes, and as we are practically unsighted there is no harm in moving about on top —indeed there is no alternative. Ploughing through the mud I find many bodies lying about still unburied. How unreal they look! They merely remind me of the gruesome newspaper pictures of the dead on battlefields. Yet looking on them now I reflect how each one had his own life, his individual hopes and fears. Individually each one was born: dead, they come back to individuality.

A fatigue-party in the mud

It is dark again. We are waiting for the mules to bring up rations. There has been little enough to do during the day, beside cheer the men up and get them to rub their feet and change their socks, and so, if possible, ward off what is miscalled frost-bite. Rain has been falling off and on all day, and once or twice a great silt of mud outside the dug-out looked as if it intended to close up

the entrance. We dug hard to prevent it, and
though the water still runs down the steps, the
mud seems to have stopped shifting.

The mules are late: but that's no wonder; what
is marvellous is that those small-footed beasts
should ever be able to drag their feet through the
miles of mud that lie between us and Ginchy. No
horses could do it. That this is a fact is now
borne out by the quartermaster-sergeant, who,
unused to marching, arrives fagged out to tell
us that the doctor's horse has slipped into a shell-
hole up to the neck and had to have his load of
rations cut from his back before he could be pulled
out. Those rations are now at the bottom of the
shell-hole. Somebody will have to go short in con-
sequence, and Rowley very properly decides that
the company in reserve must be the losers.

Mallow, who is now attached to B Company,
has his party of five-and-twenty men waiting in
the darkness and mud outside the dug-out. The
rations arrive and are apportioned: the men
loaded up with the bags and old petrol-tins filled
with water. A priceless jar of rum is given into
the charge of an N.C.O. The business of getting
the party off is not made easier by shelling which
comes presumably because a lantern carried by
the transport-party has been observed.

As soon as the ration-party has moved off,
Hardy and I parade thirty men and two sergeants
and set out for brigade headquarters in search

of sandbags. We have no guide, and after going steadily for about an hour realise we have lost our way. This is not surprising considering the country and the darkness, but we must of course find the brigade headquarters if we spend the rest of the night in search. Batteries are firing in the hollow. The men behind those gun-flashes will be able to direct us; so we make for the flashes and in time arrive at the gun-pits. An Australian battery puts us on our track.

It is no simple path. Time and again we are climbing over deep, waterlogged, disused trenches, tripping over telegraph wire, and tearing rents in our clothes on barbed strands; but before midnight we reach the deep dug-outs. There, after waiting some time, we load each of our men with as much as he can carry. Slowly we make the return journey, going well until we pass our own reserve line and encounter the four hundred yards that separate us from battalion headquarters. Here the mud is often knee-deep. The men are tired and hungry. They get stuck in the mud and have to be pulled out; but after any amount of wrenching and pulling, falling and swearing, we do get the sandbags delivered. Precisely what purpose they are to serve we cannot think, for anyone who has tried to fill sandbags with mud that is like glue knows he is performing the task of Sisyphus.

Coming back to our trenches more men get stuck, so that we form a straggling procession as

we come in. Returning to see that all have arrived,
I find Corporal Jackson half-carrying a big fellow
who has wrenched and twisted his leg. Jackson
himself is as cheerful as a cricket. It is moving, but
now unsurprising, to find this little man playing the
Good Samaritan with all the good will of his proto-
type and even more good humour. Jackson behaves
as if he liked difficulties.

Shells and mud

We have been here two endless days. Day and
night the shelling is more constant than it was at
Hébuterne, but less concentrated than at St.
George's Hill, and certainly shelling seems less
terrifying in this weather than it did when the
ground was dry. There is less noise and the area
of danger is more confined. The fellows were surprised when I said I preferred this to Hébuterne.
Of course, as far as conditions are concerned,
Hébuterne was luxury by comparison; but it mad-
dens me to stand in a perfectly constructed, sand-
bagged and revetted trench waiting for the 5.9
that will not miss. I prefer the open, where movement is possible, even if there is more metal flying
about. The more civilised the conditions, the more
intolerable shelling becomes. Honestly I would
rather be here than straying about a London street
while Zeppelins went overhead. Out here we know
we are in it up to the neck, and there is satisfaction

to be derived from that so long as activity of some kind is possible.

Mallow had a bad time with his ration-party last night. They lost their way, had two killed and two wounded, and only got about half the rations into the line. It was almost light before the party returned. Let's hope Smalley has better luck to-night, or those poor beggars up in front will be hungry. They say the mud up there is appalling.

We stand outside the dug-out watching a wonderful sunset after another wet day. Our friends the aeroplanes come out of the sunset to wish us good night. How beautiful, orderly and civilised they look above this devastation! They are our sole reminders here of a world behind this: our only visitors and the only signs of life visible from this spot. As they wheel to go, we would fain give them messages to take back to the civilised world.

Darkness falls. Shells like devils of darkness come from over the hill and spit up the mud. We dive down our rat-hole, where a candle is guttering, and express the hope that a big crump will never drop right overhead.

Cruel Fate

Our regular company-sergeant-major is taking a course in Paris. Sergeant Brown, who is acting on his behalf, comes to the mouth of the dug-out to report that a big shell dropped right in the trench, killing one man, though who it was he doesn't yet know: the body was blown to pieces. No one else was hurt. Rowley tells him to go back and find out who it was.

The sergeant has come back to the top of the dugout. He now reports that he has found the man's pay-book and identity disk, adding "so that's all right." The name is Stream.

Stream! Good God! That's the boy about whom Rowley received that letter. Only one casualty in the company all the while we've been here, and that, this boy blown to pieces so that there is literally nothing left to bury! What will it mean to the lad's mother? We feel a weight of gloom as if Fate and the Devil himself were one.

NOVEMBER

NOVEMBER

A ration-party in the mud

*H*ILL IS NOT UP ON THIS TOUR: HE remained with the rear party under Major Smythe. Hardy is in charge of his tunnellers, occupying a trench near by. It is my turn to take the ration-party up to-night, and the rations must arrive somehow, for Smalley's journey was only a little better than Mallow's. Four wounded and again rations lost.

By the way, fairly heavy casualties are occurring in the line, and to-day I had to find men from my platoon to act as extra stretcher-bearers, the regular bearers being insufficient and exhausted owing to the conditions. I asked for volunteers, and got them without the least difficulty. As might be expected, the best, but not always the most physically fit, volunteered. I should like to have shaken hands with those fellows, for they knew what they were letting themselves in for, and they went, almost shyly, without a semblance of heroics or thought of recognition.

The sergeant brings up the fatigue-party. I talk to them as they stand in the mud, waiting for the mules, telling them that every man has got to do his damnedest, because the fellows up there are short of grub, and no matter what happens every ration must be delivered. I appeal to them as good sportsmen not to let their pals down.

We must see this job through, for it is a humane one and worth doing.

Loaded and ready, we start off in single file and trudge to headquarters, where we have to report to the adjutant. 'Tis a very dark night, but luckily there is no rain. We enter the sunken road. The conditions here are terrible. The road itself has become a broad river of mud, in places two feet deep. On the right there seems to be a deep bank, and movement by it tells me there are men huddled there. They are using the bank for cover, as a trench at this level would of course be flooded. On the left is the entrance to the dug-out, and near its mouth runners, signallers and orderlies crouch together in knots to keep themselves warm. As my party has to stand in the liquid mud while I go down the dug-out to report, I hurry off, and doing so stumble over a bundle and very nearly fall head-long down the steps.

"What the devil . . .?"

"Look out, sir! That's a dead man," comes the response in injured tones. Shuddering, I realise I have kicked one of their number who has just been killed.

The scene below is palatial compared with the gruesome swamp up above. This is quite a respectable place partitioned into two rooms. It is pitiful to think there is actually plenty of accommodation down here for those poor devils shivering outside. The adjutant and then the colonel rub in the necessity of getting all the rations delivered, and I go out by another flight of steps and meet the darkness.

Now we are wading down the flooded road. This dug-out is a mark for fire, but please Heaven they will not shell us just here, for if a man were not killed outright being wounded he might easily drown. No, the luck holds. Now we are clambering up the steep side of the road and nearing the empty trenches that presumably were once the second line. I have put the sergeant in front and bring up the rear myself because I want to make dead certain that no one falls out. 'Tis devilish hard work to get through this mud: one's very joints seem as if they will part. And what's this? a man half-lying on his back with a ration-bag at his feet.

"What are you doing?"

"Sorry, sir, I'm whacked," he replies slowly in a low voice.

"Get up! Damn you! Don't you think those poor devils in the front line are whacked?"

"Sorry—I can't—I'm absolutely done. You know, sir," and here he pauses, continuing in a whispered voice, as if he were telling me a secret, "we don't get enough to eat."

This is true enough at the moment. Moreover this man is forty and not very strong; but I have sworn we would get those rations up, and the journey has hardly begun.

"Look here," I say, "if you don't get up, it's my duty to shoot you for disobeying an order. You understand? Either you get up and go on, or I shall have to shoot."

He does not stir, but after waiting a moment replies in the voice of one turning over to sleep:

"Then, sir, I'm afraid you'll have to shoot."

I'm second-best at this encounter. The monstrous absurdity of the threat makes me feel a fool. Cursing, I pick up his ration-bag and hasten after the disappearing file to find the men standing alongside a communication-trench debating the possibility of going up it. Already three of them are attempting this, but they haven't gone a dozen yards before they are stuck fast and give us much to do to pull them out. We will have no more of that, but keep to the line of the trench, and when we believe we are approaching the end, crawl away to the right and drop into the front line over the parados.

We move on, but fearfully slowly, slipping and sliding about, circumventing shell-holes and troubled most of all by dead bodies that look as if they have been thrown out of the communication-trench. They lie about, singly or in groups, stretched in every conceivable attitude. The living men have an innate respect for the dead and avoid touching a corpse, or even walking over it, if possible.

At last we come to the front-line trench and one by one the men fling themselves into it. Shots are fired, but by the time I am in I know that no one has been hit. This trench is just a great gully, the bottom of it so deep in mud that the only way to get along is to move straddle-wise. The men holding the line are perched up on the slope of the parapet wherever there is a foothold. Toiling along, it is soon apparent that half my men are stuck in the bottom of the trench and can get no farther. Lightlier weighted, I pass them till I come to the head of the file, and then send back word that the rations are to be handed along from man to man while I report to Captain Wilson.

He sits crouched in a hole in the parados hardly big enough to contain him. He has a ground-sheet flap over the front of the hole, but it does not prevent the candlelight shining through chinks at the side.

"By Jove, Wilson! this is a rough show."

"Yes, awful, isn't it? But we're coming out tomorrow. You brought all the rations? That's good! Do you think you could take a couple of casualties back with you? I've two boys hurt. They can walk, but they can't get back without help, and I've no one to send."

"Right-o!"

"See the sergeant-major about them, will you? I won't come out; one of my feet has gone groggy with the wet. Yes, it's beastly painful and I shall have as much as I can do to get out to-morrow. Pleased you've got all the rations up: we've been very short."

He smiles his friendly old smile and pats me on the shoulder like a father as I drop the flap.

Good-bye, Wilson!

I do not know that this is the last time I shall see him: that he will go into hospital for a while with his foot: that (owing to his age, long service in the trenches, and sickness) he will be offered a job at the base which, though a newly married man, he will decline, saying "he knows the men so well now"; and that finally he, the best company-commander I ever met, will be killed in the trenches, dying without honours. But so it is to be.

After seeing the sergeant-major, who sends along the wounded boys, I go back and find most of the men have extricated themselves and are lying behind the back of the trench waiting to return. But there is a lad here, Bird, the fat boy of Hardy's platoon, stuck fast and unable to move. Obtaining a shovel, we lay it across the trench, tell him to kneel on it and pull. He kneels and the shovel sinks, but Bird remains if anything now deeper in the mud. He looks, "I told you so," and stands motionless as if to prove the hopelessness of his case.

Fidgeting on parade is Bird's especial vice. He cannot fidget now. "Well, Bird," say I, "you're not on parade, but you're standing still at last." He sees no humour in the remark, and I am afraid he is going to start blubbering. Something must be done. Shovels are useless: the only thing is to drag the pug away from his legs with one's hands, and this I proceed to do, encouraging him to pull as I loosen one leg. After twenty minutes of this business I get sick of it, and still more sick of his feeble efforts to help himself. I give it up.

"There it is, if you can't get out, we shall have to leave you. You'll have to stay there till the rest of the company comes out, and," I add vindictively, "we've brought no rations up here for *you*."

He looks at me aghast.

"Then I'll have nothing to eat!"

"No, nothing."

The horror of this prospect puts demons of energy into him. He pulls and pulls till it looks as if his foot will come off; but at last, with a mighty squelch, it appears. The rest is easy. Bird is saved by his belly.

Two or three of my men have gone on with the casualties: the rest of us now follow. Halfway back I meet a young subaltern belonging to one of the regiments in our brigade. He is in great distress. He has lost his men—the whole platoon. He left them in a trench all right while he went back to a dug-out to get some cigarettes, and when he returned the whole lot had gone. What do I think he ought to do? Of course, he'll be court-martialled for leaving them. Will I give evidence that he was honestly trying to find them again?

I suggest he must have mistaken the trench and that they are still there. No. He is certain about it. They have "done a bunk" and he'll be "for it." I do my best to console him all the way back to battalion headquarters, where I have to report again. There I leave him.

At the bottom of the dug-out stands the colonel, smothered in mud from head to foot, a pole still in his hand. He has been trying, the adjutant tells me, to get up to the front line; but the mud was too much for him.

Out again, we lug ourselves over the last long lap. Our journey of three thousand yards started at seven: it is now two o'clock. I stumble down into the little dug-out on legs that feel as if they were made in two pieces of cast iron. What matters? We have delivered the rations without a casualty.

The deserter

The quartermaster-sergeant has brought up rare news of Sergeant Griffen, who was my platoon-sergeant at Hébuterne. While we were at Méaulte he was sent with about half a dozen men to rail-head, then near Mametz, to unload bombs. He had to make billeting and rationing arrangements, for himself and the men, with the town-major of Méaulte; so that, for the time being, he and his party were detached from the regiment. Apparently he went up with the men once and returned, reporting to the town-major that the bombs had not arrived and he had been instructed to wait at Méaulte. There he hung about for a week, drawing rations for the men and himself all the time. At the end of the week the men began to suspect something was wrong and at the same time Sergeant Griffen disappeared. The men returned to find the battalion in the line and themselves apprehended for desertion. They explained their case to the C.O., who withdrew the charge and sent them on to the trenches. Meantime it appears that Griffen donned the uniform of a sergeant-major, forged a cheque for a thousand francs, and was last heard of at Amiens. Quite obviously he is asking to be shot if he is caught, and I would not stir a finger to save him; for if he is skunk enough to want to dodge these trenches himself, that doesn't excuse him for very nearly having half a dozen men court-martialled for desertion. It sounds as if the man must have gone mad; but knowing him, I suspect that he guessed what these trenches would be like and thought he would take his chances elsewhere. I doubt if he escapes.

Nothing doing

Like the prospect of paradise is the thought
that we are coming out of these trenches to-night;
but now at midday come tales from the company
runners of our wounded lying about through in-
sufficiency of stretcher-bearers and want of someone to organise them. This is obviously my job,
and I tell Rowley I should like to take it on. Rowley says it can't be done: we might be wanted at
a moment's notice in case of trouble. I point out
that the conditions make that highly improbable:
that it's absurd we should be hanging about doing
nothing while some of our fellows are being
worked to death and others dying owing to delay.
I ask him if he'll let me go to the colonel about it,
seeing that I reckon myself an expert at first-aid.
Rowley declines, and I am much disgruntled. He
might at least let the question of military necessity
be decided by the C.O.

Coming out

Heaven knows where we shall finish up to-night!
We have trailed the whole length of those rickety
duck-boards, marched as a company to Trônes
Wood, and now here we are, marching and
counter-marching in the darkness as if nobody had
an idea where we were bound for. I trust we are
not merely manœuvring to fill up time, for to a
man we are fagged out. Smalley says we are looking for a rest-camp where we can get hot tea

before going back to Mansel Copse. For my part, I should like to lie here on the hillside for the next two days. We are then due to return to those unspeakable trenches.

Rest

Back in the old tent with the smoky brazier. It is Sunday. Thank God, I'm not orderly-officer. I trust no one will ask me to move for the next twelve hours. I'm too tired yet even to get clean. Lord! What a march! The men are still straggling in. About three-quarters of the company arrived with the column this morning, and I honestly believe half my platoon would have dropped out if it hadn't been for Jackson, who simply wouldn't let them stop singing. That little man is a marvel. I have never seen such pluck.

Trench-feet

I have been talking to one of my stretcher-bearers. He has a foot swollen to three times its normal size: a great shapeless bright pink lump. He has been stretcher-bearing over that awful ground almost the whole of the four days. Changing his socks did no good: the water came in over the tops of his boots as soon as he started bearing again. He is an excellent fellow and genuinely disappointed at having to leave us. Poor beggar! I shall be surprised if he doesn't lose that foot.

Back to the mud

We have tramped through Montauban, Bernafay, Trônes Wood, Guillemont, Ginchy and across the plain again. We have passed our old trenches and the battalion dug-out and now stand, at midnight, stuck in the communication-trench. There has been no rain for two days; we therefore hoped to find this trench passable. Rowley is at the head of the file. I wonder what he is doing, for we have not advanced for nearly an hour, and still we do not move. My patience gives out. I climb on top and go up alongside the row of sacking-covered helmets till I come to Rowley standing at the junction of the two trenches. I am kneeling down talking to him in low tones, when "Phut!" "Ping!"—one shot falls short in the mud and another glances off my tin hat. In double time I heave myself over into the mud.

Whoever it is we are relieving, they have gone already. The trench is empty. In the watery moonlight it appears a very ghostly place. Corpses lie along the parados, rotting in the wet: every now and then a booted foot appears jutting over the trench. The mud makes it all but impassable, and now, sunk in up to the knees, I have the momentary terror of never being able to pull myself out. Such horror gives frenzied energy, and I tear my legs free and go on. Turning sharply round a bend I come upon a fearsome sight. Deep water lies in a descending right-angle of the trench, and at

arm's length from me a body has fallen face down-
ward in the water, barring the way. Shall I push
the body aside and wade, chancing the depth of
the water, or shall I get out on top and double
across the corner? There is a sunken road here:
that is why the water stands, and ten to one a
German sniper is hiding on the forward slope
below. If I try the water it may prove too deep;
even if it isn't, I shall be wet to the thighs, and
there are four days to go; besides that body. . . .
If I go over the top and the sniper hits, what a
kindness he might do me! I am up now, running
and dodging. Twice the sniper fires, but I am
more troubled to dodge the bodies than the
sniper's aim. Now over, and slap into the trench;
and that is past, with not only a whole but a dry
skin.

Rain and mud

Rain, rain, rain! It has rained all day. We are
all in the trench at last, though some of the men
remained stuck on the way till long after daylight.
While the trenches are in this condition we can
neither get to the Germans nor they to us. Both
sides are glued where they stand, so that Heaven
alone knows what purpose we serve here, or
whether we shall ever get out again. Like so many
grotesque monuments, the men sit huddled under
their ground-sheets at their places beneath the
parapet. I wonder how many of those rifles would

fire? I wonder how they are ever going to get them clean again? To move fifty yards along the trench is, at present, half an hour's work. If it goes on raining . . .

The runners have the worst time. We've two splendid fellows who will go anywhere that is humanly possible. It takes them hours to get to and from battalion headquarters, and they risk their lives every time. They have brought back chits instructing us to get the men to work clearing the trenches and putting the place in repair. Noah might as well have given such instructions to the dove. When it stops raining we shall see what can be done. At present, even to move is only to churn up the pug and make further movement impossible. We simply haven't the tools to clear this stuff; shovels are perfectly useless.

Rowley replies, smiling grimly as he writes, that the instructions are noted. I foresee trouble here, and beg him to be frank with the colonel and tell him clearly how matters stand. Ask him to come and see for himself.

The whole duty of a soldier, as Rowley understands it, is to receive orders and carry them out —as and when possible. In vain do I point out that nobody besides ourselves *can* know what this place is like. Rowley is adamant, and the "eye-wash" goes its way.

We have been here twelve hours and have not yet got into touch with the battalion on our right.

There's an impassable gap between us. At night it may be possible to get out in front and go round; but even that is very doubtful.

All this wants saying elsewhere. I cannot believe Rowley does well in keeping this kind of thing from the colonel.

Meantime here we sit, Smalley, Rowley and myself, in a hole in the parados, six by three by three. German rifles and their bayonets, covered by German ground-sheets, serve for a roof, and another ground-sheet makes a flap that covers us in front down to the knees. Our feet stick out in the mud and are sometimes uncomfortably trodden on. I came into the trench with a nice long Burberry, long enough to keep one's knees dry, but by the time we arrived it was caked to the waist, so I have cut off the skirt and it now looks like an Eton jacket with frills.

The limit

Rain has been falling almost continuously for two days, and if it goes on much longer we shall indeed leave these trenches, being washed out. Chits continue to come detailing the work expected of us, and Rowley continues to reply that instructions are noted; but little or nothing is done, for the simple reason that the Deity has not yet constructed men able to make or repair trenches when the earth at every step holds them immovable.

Last night Smalley and a sergeant went out to get in touch with the regiment on our right, but after being half-drowned they had to return. There are portions of the earth's surface that under some conditions remain impassable by un-aided man, even though he learns from his com-manding-officer half a dozen times a day that it is imperative they should be passed. That is the fact; but I am sure this pretence that we are doing the impossible is a tragic game.

Shelling is sporadic. Soon after dark last night we had a lot of shells uncomfortably near. Luckily not one fell in the trench, and so far all our casualties here have occurred through sniping. Last night the ration-party coming up lost its officer, shot through the head, and a fellow in my platoon and two others in the company have been killed in the same way. We should like to get at those snipers, but with the ground like this it would only be suicide to send patrols out into no-man's land. This is where a retiring enemy scores.

Hill came up with a message from the second line this evening reporting about a dozen casual-ties back there. He was wet to the thighs. Half the officers of the battalion seem to have gone sick.

Thank goodness I brought six pairs of socks.

Morning and evening we make the men take off their boots and rub their feet; but it isn't much good: they simply cannot keep them warm or dry under such conditions, and some of them are already badly frost-bitten.

This is the very limit of endurance.

In front of le Transloy

Thank Heaven it has stopped raining at last! The sun actually shines, and for the first time in three days we can really see where we are. We have parties of men at work trying to drain the trench; incidentally the squad under Jackson seems to have done the most useful work. The sentries are still trying to get their rifles clean.

There's le Transloy, 1500 yards away. There's the sugar-refinery, and in front the cemetery. How peaceful and calm it all looks in the sunshine! Gazing over here, who could imagine what a hell this place has been? Now there's no firing it seems absurd to stay here. Why don't we walk over the fields and explore the village that looks so inviting? You can bet the Germans are feeling the same. Why don't we all get out and walk away?

We seem to be here under the constraint of some malevolent idiot. In this sunshine it seems impossible to believe that at any minute we in this trench, and they in that, may be blown to bits by shells fired from guns at invisible distances by hearty fellows who would be quite ready to stand you a drink if you met them face to face. What base, pathetic slaves we are to endure such

idiocy! No doubt it's good to fight when indignation and hatred boil up as they did in 1914.
But these passions have long since spent themselves. Why are we fighting still?

We are compelled. We have endowed machin-
ery with the power once confined to a man's right
arm, and now the machine continues to function
long after our natural impulses have spent themselves. That's what makes this war so ghastly.
It is machine-made. Even our opinion is machine-
made by a press suborned with fear; and we who
do the fighting have no say in when the fight shall
cease. Man seems to have become the slave of
his own power of organisation. If all the machin-
ery of war were now suddenly taken from our
hands, I am certain the war would stop at once.

Pork and beans

Of all people entitled to praise in these times
I give the palm to the army commissariat. True
they cannot feed five thousand on five loaves and
two fishes, but after that miracle theirs comes
second. Consider it. We have been wandering
about in a foreign country for four months, and
never till this moment have we known what it
is to feel really short of food. When I remember
that this battalion is one of thousands similarly
mobile, and when I see the conditions under which
we ask so punctually not only for our daily bread,

but our regular meals, I marvel at the organisation which can respond promptly to such a demand.

Our principal food in the trenches is, of course, bully beef and bread, falling seldom to biscuits. But this is by no means all we have. Often enough there is that excellent tin of cooked meat and vegetables known familiarly as "Maconachie": there is tea and sugar, and lately we have had plentiful supplies of good Australian jam, which came as a pleasant change from the nondescript variety known as "Tickler."

At the moment I am reminded of these blessings by their absence. Yet even now there is half a loaf going. It has suffered too many hardships since it left the bakers to make it look appetising; and muddy and wet, it must wait till we see what happens to-night before it can be sure of reaching a human interior. Still, there it is. And water? There is still a drop in the bottom of the petrol-tin.

Oh, this water! The taste of water impregnated with petrol will carry me back here if I live for ever. It is a nauseous taste, and no doubt someone ought to be hanged for not washing out the spirit before adding our water. Still, it quenches thirst.

And then there's rum. Rum of course is our chief great good. The Ark of the Covenant was never borne with greater care than is bestowed upon the large stone rum-jars in their passage through this wilderness. The popularity of rum increases, till the hour when it is served tends to become a moment of religious worship. After the divine pattern, its celebration is administered by priests in the presence of higher dignitaries. When these priests happen to be old-time N.C.O.s, they want watching, or the communicants are apt to go short, to the degradation of the priests.

There are men so devout they live for rum. I honestly believe some I know would commit suicide if the rum ration were withdrawn. And in truth the rum is good—fine, strong, warming stuff—the very concentrated essence of army-council wisdom.

But while I sit in my mud-hole dreaming of rum, a miracle of generosity happens. Robinson, a quiet stretcher-bearer who looks as if he followed the plough in times of peace, comes up to me and, with a great shy smile, asks me if I would like "this"—this being an unopened tin of Heinz's Pork and Beans. He protests he does not want it.

Permit me now to depart from the praise of rum, which all men worship, and to become lyrical upon a height where few will follow. Pork and beans shall have its song of honour. What if the beans are many and the pork is far between! What if the label on the tin should read BEANS and Pork! Hunger shall prompt the muse.

Seated to-day in this mud-hole,
I am weary and ill at ease,
For the aching void of a stomach
Trembles like aspen leaves;
When a stretcher-bearer named Robinson
(Long may he live in bliss!)
Comes up with a tin of treasure
And says, "Can you do with this?"

I thank him with great profusion
And would readily share my delight
With Rowley, who's also hungry,
But he turns up his nose at the sight;
And Smalley and even Castlereagh
Reply quite emphatically, "No";
So alone I will light me a candle
And prepare me my great beano.

By the light of a single candle
I am toasting the jolly lot,
Till, by dint of a little patience,
The contents are piping hot;
And now, like an Eastern monarch
Surrounded by all his queens,
I shall slowly and solemnly dine at
A banquet of pork and beans.

It may be the years will bring me
A place in the Lord Mayor's Show,
With a feast of the pheasants that follow
In the place where fat aldermen go;
But if ever I get back to Blighty
(So long as I have the means)
I shall keep in my larder a tinful
Of Robinson's Pork and Beans.

The broken plane

A solitary German plane is flying over towards Gueudecourt. "Archies" are making their white smoke-circles round it, when it begins to drop and I see one of its wings spinning like a feather high above it. The broken butterfly itself turns round and round as it flutters to the ground, looking as if it will come to earth quite restfully. It drops out of sight; but suddenly a sheet of flame leaps up, and we realise that all that soft fluttering was only the deceitful prelude to terrible death.

Luck

Turning round from gazing over the fields before le Transloy, Rowley and I are horrified to see two of our runners coming down from the crest of the rise behind us, walking in the bright sunlight, visible to the enemy down to their feet, and looking for all the world as if they think they are out for a stroll in the country. They have lost their way. Every minute we expect to see them drop, but on they come, nearer and nearer. We try to signal to them; but either they do not understand us, or they think this is the second line; for they stroll on, right up to us, and are getting into the trench before they realise what has happened. Not a shot is fired!

A Turkish bath

I have been out in front to-night trying to get across to the regiment on our right to whom we can now signal, though the gap has never been closed. I could not get across and am soaked.

There has been pretty heavy shelling going **on**: we can see the flash of the gun that fires on us out of Bapaume, and the moments between the flash and the shaking of the trench are terribly nervous ones; but our luck has held. The Australians behind us have also been firing heavily. Hungry and tired and wet, Smalley, Rowley and I have just wrapped our cold legs and wet feet in one parcel of Burberry, hoping for a Turkish-bath effect that will enable us to sleep.

The old soldier

We slept all right till the ration-party came cluttering in right on top of us. Some of them had drunk a good ration of rum before they started, and when they arrived they were rowdy and indifferent to cursing. Possibly as a result of their noise, shelling started again. This sobered them; but daylight came too soon for them to go back, so we have entertained them for the day. One of the party, Sawyer, an old soldier, has been alternately an anxiety and an amusement. He is a man who has been with the battalion since its formation, and seen service in the South African War. These trenches have been too much for him.

Falling asleep this morning, he lay for a long while in a state of something like coma. As time went on we became alarmed and tried to wake him, wondering what we should do if he failed to rouse himself before we were relieved. He was not drunk; but wet and exposure seemed to have numbed his brain as well as his limbs. We rubbed him, shook him, pummelled him, and shouted into his ear, for a long time without effect. At last he stirred himself a little and then proceeded to deliver a short speech full of self-gratulation and pride at being the oldest soldier in the regiment. Having wasted his strength in this eloquence, he promptly fell asleep again. Again we rubbed and pummelled, and again he repeated his oration and feel asleep. This happened three or four times, but gradually a drowsy general consciousness returned, and now we only hope it will continue till dusk, when he is to be the first man to leave the trenches. Rowley has abandoned the idea of going out *via* the communication-trench, which is certainly impassable. As the animals entered the Ark, we shall go out over the back of the trench, scuttle a hundred yards, crawl over the crest and make for the duck-boards.

This morning, soon after daybreak, Perkins, a tall dark man of my platoon, was fatally wounded while on sentry. He must have lifted his head an inch too high: a sniper got him with a bullet through the top of his helmet. Poor fellow! He thought he was only wounded and was pleased as a child at the idea of going home. Gradually his breathing became heavy: he lapsed into unconsciousness and died in the trench an hour ago. There was no possibility of getting him back to the doctor. Thus comedy and tragedy have been jostling each other all day.

Exit the old soldier

Old Sawyer is still awake. For about the fourth time Rowley is giving him his instructions:

"You see, you go up the ladder, then crawl for about fifty yards. Then nip up the hill till you're about twenty yards from the top. Crawl again till you're right over. Then take to your heels, and the best of luck. And don't stop going till you get off the duck-boards. You understand? Now tell me what you've got to do."

Sawyer repeats what he remembers and is duly corrected. "Right-o! Now you're off. And keep going."

With a little help he clambers up the steps, and we watch the huddled figure moving, slowly as a tortoise, among the pitiful dead bodies. He becomes blurred in the dusk. We turn away, congratulating ourselves on having got him to go. The next moment someone says he has stopped crawling and fallen asleep. Peering through the dusk we are convinced the old fellow is out of sight and that the motionless form indicated is a corpse, when, to our dismay, it begins to move, to turn round and crawl towards us! Back comes old Sawyer, as slowly as he had gone, inch by inch, till at last he regains the trench.

Rowley meets him.

"Why the devil didn't you go on? You were more than half-way."

"I were too tired, sir, to go any farther. So I thought I'd better come back and have a rest."

Rowley remarks to me that the next time we push him off we'll have a man behind him with a bayonet and give him orders not to let the old fellow stop this side of the Channel.

The relief

The moon is getting up. The men are going out in twos when silhouetted forms appear on top of the rise. It is the relieving company coming over all at once in extended order. Shots are fired and some of the shadowy forms drop. The next minute the trench is invaded, and our successors begin to "take over." While I am waiting in the mud-hole I overhear one of them talking to himself as he struggles to move down the trench. Every word is punctuated by the prodigious effort of drawing a leg out of the mud.

"Lloyd George," he growls, "said—this—was a fight—to the finish. The b—— had better—come out here—and finish it."

Rowley and I are the last to go. For the past

two days, worried by our plight and the chits from headquarters, he has been refusing food and relying on whisky; now he is as weak as a kitten, and when he falls is hardly persuaded to go on. We are sighted and shot at more than once, but the old luck holds. Struggling over the crest, we get out of direct range and sit for a long time by the side of a shell-hole which has a body lying in it. Then I persuade him to come along, and slowly we continue till we reach headquarters' dug-out where the adjutant takes him down and gives him food and a hot drink.

Outside in the mud and the dark, I am talking to three of my volunteer stretcher-bearers when whiz-bangs come over, dropping among us. We disperse, but when the firing is over I can only find one of them and he is wounded.

Rowley returns. We pick up Hardy and together tramp the endless duck-boards. Posts have now been established, just off the duck-boards, where hot drinks are to be had, and but for these I question whether Rowley would have finished the journey to the rest-camp at Montauban.

"L'esprit c'est la force"

It is early morning before we find the camp on the hill. As we enter wearily, ominous shoutings and groanings come from all directions. These sounds tell the tale. The men are crying out with the pain in their feet. But there is nothing to be done now and, dog-tired, I am on the point of dropping into a tarpaulin-covered hole, when I remember my platoon. What can I do for them? Well, at least I ought to see how they are. Wandering round alone I come on a coke-fire burning at the end of one of the shelters. A dark figure stands by tending it. It is Jackson.

"Hullo! What are you doing?"

"Only looking to this fire, sir. I thought if I kept it going on this side, the wind 'd blow the heat through."

"Where are they?"

"They're all in there. There's only Collins and Roberts bad. The sergeant's pretty fair. He's inside. Shall I fetch him?"

"No. That's all right. How about yourself? Where are you going to sleep? Is there any room there?"

"No, sir, but I shall be all right. There's several of them want looking to. I'd as soon be here. I'm getting dry."

I bid him good night, and go back to the officers' shelter, thinking of heroism and wherein it consists. This is the unostentatious kind. Here's a wisp of a man with a permanently troublesome knee. He has just come from trenches, said to be worse than Ypres in 1914, where he has done two men's work, besides helping crocks out of the mud, supporting them and carrying their rifles. Under the foulest conditions his spirits have never flagged. I have heard him whistling when no other bird on earth would sing; and now, when by all the laws of Nature he ought to have dropped half-dead, he has appointed himself to the rôle of Florence Nightingale, and has not even left himself room to lie down. I cannot sleep for thinking of him. The Lady of the Lamp. The Gentleman of the Brazier.

A sorry sight

Here's a pitiable sight! Half a battalion being taken off in G.S. wagons because they are unable to walk. Many cannot even get into the wagons by themselves, and it is hard work carrying and lifting them in. And there they sit and stand, like victims in the tumbrils on their way to the guillotine. Some will be unloaded at the hut near Mametz, to which the rest of the battalion is moving; others will go on to the field-hospital. There's Hill and Smalley standing together in the corner of one wagon. I must go across and wish them good-bye and good luck.

This is the last time I shall see Hill, who has yet to go home, get well, transfer to the Flying Corps (knowing his feet would never stand another winter here) and be killed flying over the German lines.

The adjutant comes round, going from shelter to shelter, inquiring if there is any officer there who can walk. I tell him I can.

"Then you're for a sniping course," he replies. "You'll start to-morrow. Take your servant, and get to Pont Noyelles as best you can."

Well, well! There are many ways of choosing a marksman: eyes, hand and nerve must be considered; but this is the first time I have ever heard of one being chosen for his feet.

Meantime we parade for the short march to Mametz. Out of a company of over two hundred we can only muster fifty-two, and I note that one of them is Jackson and another Rowley—sportsmen both: they will stick it out to the end.

There is not more than two miles to it, but this is the most painful march I have ever made. We are tired out: the road is constantly blocked, and the repeated halts on loose granite, which is like glass to our tender feet, cause frenzied and impotent swearing. A little more of this and we should all drop down and cry.

How much farther? Ah! There are the huts. We are nearly there. Thank God, the camp at last. Which hut? Which hut? Not this one? Is that it? The right hut at last. Now a valise. Oh, what comfort rest on the floor can be to limbs that are really tired! And here's the sainted quartermaster-sergeant bringing round hot tea and waiting on us like a nurse.

No, thanks—nothing to eat, only sleep—sleep —oceans of it.

On the road to Amiens

They say it's about seven miles from Pont Noyelles to Amiens; anyway it will be a good walk. The commandant of the Telescopic Sniping School, out of pity for my mud-stained condition, has given me special leave to go to Amiens; so here I am on the road alone, in search of pants and puttees, pyjamas and most of all a shampoo, for it will take a good barber to get the mud out of my hair. Since I joined the battalion nearly four months ago, this is the first time I have been away from it for a day. It seems quite strange to be walking alone in a country road. I wonder where the battalion is now? This must be the first hour I have been really alone since I came to France. It is a pleasure. I can stuff my hands in my short "British-warm," the cane sticking out at any angle it pleases, and almost forget the war. O Lord! If only I were back in England for an hour! Well, leave will come—in time—perhaps.

Less than three days ago we were in those trenches. It's hardly credible. The weather has changed, and after sharp frost there's a sprinkling of snow on the ground, making the countryside white and beautiful. All the same, I hope the frost doesn't last. I'm too pinched and achey in the bones for hard weather. By the way, the fellows who followed us into those trenches must be glad of this frost. Two hundred odd cases of trench-

feet it would have saved us had it come a week
ago.

Somebody ought to be shot for keeping us up
there four days at a time without any precautions
against trench-feet. I wonder whether the culprit
will ever bear the onus of that mistake. Very
likely we shall never know who he is.

I hope Rowley will get my recommendation
for Jackson through. If ever a man did deserve
recognition there's a case. And if, as Hardy says
he is doing, Rowley puts one through for me,
what shall I do about it? This I know: that I can
lay my hand on my heart and say without cant
or false modesty that I have done nothing to
deserve it. Moreover *we* all know *why* he has done
it. Didn't he vow when we met a rag-tag regiment at Halloy, with almost every officer in the
battalion wearing an M.C., that somebody besides
"those blighters" would be up for decorations
next time we came out? I trust I shouldn't have
the face to wear it; but it puts me in difficulty,
for to refuse point-blank might be to let Rowley
down rather badly. Let's hope the colonel cuts
it out.

Those gunners in their car seem to know how
to do themselves pretty well. If they are going
into Amiens, they might give me a lift. Oh, luck!
They are stopping and signalling to me to come
along.

The sniping course

This school is quite good fun. It is run by elderly officers who have Bisley reputations and, like all men who are really keen on some particular branch of knowledge, they know how to make the subject interesting. If only I felt perfectly fit and the weather were not so cold, it would be thoroughly enjoyable.

We have a lecture at 8.30: spend the morning on the range: come back for lunch: then on to the range again at 2, and back again for another lecture at 5.30. The course only lasts a week and there's an examination at the end of it. It's rather ironic that I should be on such a course, for we haven't a telescopic rifle in the battalion.

We are a mixed company, Highlanders, Australians, a Guardsman, and none above the rank of captain. The Australians are very characteristic, good-natured, devil-may-care fellows, a little inclined to brag (as is customary with all men belonging to nations of recent civilisation) and good soldiers in a tight corner, I haven't a doubt. The Guards' officer makes an amusing study in contrast. He is fair, sleek, rather bald, wears a monocle and is in other respects perfectly turned out. I wondered at first how he would sort with the Australians, but in spite of his superficial manner, he is neither a snob nor a mere dandy. Best of all he has an excellent sense of humour. They get along famously, and before the end of the

week the Guardsman will be the most popular
man here.

The course, which is principally concerned with
the use and care of telescopic-sighted rifles, includes instruction in the employment and detec-
tion of camouflage and, of course, distance-judg-
ing. Firing with a telescopic sight is a refinement
of marksmanship, and in the realm of sport is a
fine art which anybody with a good eye and steady
hands might well prefer to golf. It is pleasant
and flattering to be able to hit an object invisible
to the naked eye. It is fascinating to discover the
characteristics of a particular rifle; and judging
the strength and direction of wind is a nice specu-
lative study.

I begin to see that war entails many employ-
ments which are wholly enjoyable provided a certain part of the imagination is atrophied. The
great seductive enjoyment of war, outside the
infantry ranks, is the sense of power it confers.
By means of finely adjusted guns and the use of
high explosives, the maximum of effect can be
produced by the minimum of effort, and this ap-
peals to a childish instinct latent in everyone. "You
press the button and we do the rest." The appeal
to this instinct will sell millions of cameras in times
of peace; but what is the wonder of pressing a
button and seeing a photograph compared with
the wonder of pulling a string and seeing as the
result a dump go up perhaps five miles away?

Every sport, if you come to analyse it, depends largely upon its power of producing a big effect with apparently small cause, whether the power resides in the ace of hearts, the thickness of a cricket-bat, or the responsiveness of a golf-ball to fine timing. In war this apparent disproportionate relation between cause and effect, which confers its flattering and enjoyable sense of power upon the player, is seen at its highest. Hence, from this standpoint, war is king of sports. Only imagination can spoil the game.

I see that most clearly when, having thoroughly enjoyed practice upon a target, I begin to feel squeamish on being told that firing low is a mistake because the head is the most vulnerable part of a man. Bull's-eyes on a target are a pleasure; but when the power to make them becomes applied and we are told of the wonderful logs kept by certain snipers who recorded their bag each day as if human heads were of less account than pheasants, then a gruesome sense of mean inhumanity begins to assert itself and I think with comparative esteem of the cannibal chief and his scalps. I prefer his honesty.

Of course one does not mention this here, knowing it would be regarded as humanitarian rot. Nevertheless, it seems to me that as imagination is the great distinguishing characteristic of man, to which he has attained late in his growth, it is not improbable that when this quality in him has grown a little stronger, not only will war be impossible to man, but he will find higher uses for his energy in peace than the blind and pitiless self-assertion which at present makes so many of his activities forms of war.

Sick

We have finished the course, and the officers attending it have gone into Amiens for a farewell dinner. I am sorry not to be there; but my "innerds," which have been troublesome since we left the trenches, have collapsed and left me limp: fit only to sit over the fire in this lonely white-washed room. It may be the effect of drinking too much petrol or—faithless thought—could it be those BEANS? No. I'm afraid it's the water, for I am told that others, who have no passion for beans, have been similarly affected lately.

I'm curious to see what has happened to the battalion, but otherwise sorry this little school is breaking up. We have been good company and enjoyed it, work and all.

Last night we had a mock court-martial. One of our number got up late and missed the range, so we charged him with "malingering," and formed a court over which the Guardsman presided. It was a good rag. The prisoner was remanded for medical examination at 3 a.m.; but nobody woke early enough to carry it out.

Comfort in Amiens

It is Sunday in Amiens. A lorry brought half a dozen of us in from Pont Noyelles. We are spending the night at hotels here and rejoining our regiments first thing to-morrow. We went to the cathedral this afternoon and, after wandering round, attended part of a service. Let's hope nothing befalls this lovely place. It is heavily sand-bagged on the east and southern sides, though the protection looks trivial.

Coming away I met the subaltern who had lost his platoon in the mud about a fortnight ago, and was in such mortal fear of being court-martialled. I was interested to hear what had happened, for he now looked cheerful enough. He explained, rather shamefacedly, that as a matter of fact his men had never left their places: he had merely lost his way and mistaken the trench which he found again next morning.

What extraordinary luxury it is to be waited on in a hotel: to have hot baths and food served on white tablecloths with a sufficiency of cutlery! Best of all is the relief from life by order. To be one's own master, just for an hour or two, is to me relaxation beyond belief. Probably most men do not let the trivial responsibilities of regimental life hang with such absurd weight upon them. To me, just to forget time is a delicious rest.

To-night Amiens seems all jewellers and restaurants. Many of the other shops are closed, but these seem to be doing great business. From the worst trenches to a French jeweller's is a big stride. Their common multiple, I suppose, is—us.

Now for the enormous ease of a French bed with its invariable box-mattress! French bed-makers should go to England: they could teach our manufacturers of wire racks a lot.

White sheets and a pillow for the first time for ages!

Out of favour

Lord preserve us!—for it is certain no one else will.

After jogging along early this morning in the suburban train from Amiens, I climbed the hill leading to the village of Camps-en-Amienois (about ten miles west of Amiens) where the battalion was said to be in billets. I was still feeling seedy, but pleased at the thought that I had lasted out the course at Pont Noyelles and was still fit enough to keep going. As I hammered along the road I wondered if I should be given charge of the battalion snipers and whether I could pre-suade the quartermaster to set about getting us telescopic rifles.

I found Rowley in an estaminet with a collection of chits on his table, which he was very busy answering. I thought he looked blear-eyed and sounded very despondent. He soon explained why.

The battalion, and not only the battalion, but

the whole brigade, is in a very bad odour with the divisional command because of what happened, or rather did not happen, in front of le Transloy. The programme for us there apparently ran something like this: "If fine, capture German trenches: if wet, do intensive work in your own."

Well, it was *wet,* and we did *not* do intensive work. Reason given for this negligence: it was wet.

Personally I see in all this the bitter and disastrous end of failing to acquaint the commanding-officer with the truth about the conditions. But I think I now know the progress of army displeasure.

Corps-commander strafes divisional-commander, divisional-commander strafes brigadier, brigadier strafes colonel of regiment, colonel strafes company-commander, captains strafe platoon-commanders, and subalterns work it off where and when they can, usually on sergeants and men. It's a game of "Touch-last," or it might be called "Fixing the Responsibility."

The colonel is "going." The brigadier is "going": the colonel to a reduced rank in another of the regiment's battalions: the brigadier home —perhaps to guard the East coast. I should like to be going with the brigadier if half the vials of wrath Rowley predicts are to be emptied. But subalterns do not go home when they belong to regiments that are reputed to have let down their

commanding-officers. Their leave is withheld, and
they are kept for intensive training, frequent inspections, and permitted to remain on duty all
day and a good part of the night, in the hope
that by some outstanding exploit in the trenches,
next time they go there, they may retrieve the
battalion's good name.

So it was for this that we hung on under conditions which no Red Tab will ever know (seeing
that not one ever came as far as battalion headquarters), conditions which the colonel himself
only surmised, seeing that he never managed
(though, to give him his due, I happen to know
he tried very hard) to reach the trenches. For
this we packed our haversacks with socks, and,
more by force of will than by any gift of strength,
managed to keep out of hospital, while those who
have arrived there are enjoying the comforts of
wounded heroes.

Well, well! However much want of fore-
thought there may have been in sending men up
to those trenches for practically ten days on end
without special precautions against trench-feet,
sheer bad luck is the cause of nearly all our
troubles. We went into the line just when the
weather finally broke down. Those trenches had
been getting bad: we happened on them just at
the cracking-point; and since provision was not
made against that moment, someone must bear
the blame.

Fate is grimly ironic in time of war. She speaks through the lips of two-headed Janus, as many a good officer has found to his cost. When we left Hébuterne the battalion was congratulated in divisional orders upon its fine work. We did less than our duty there. Now, after giving all we had, after countless minor heroisms (those stretcher-bearers and cases like Jackson's), after endurance such as I fancy some of us will be physically incapable of repeating, we are—well, to put it succinctly, "in the soup." The two-headed one looks on us with the sour face. Perhaps with less reason he will turn another face another day. Meantime we must grin and bear it, or just bear it, if the grin sticks. What really gets one's goat is the thought that these men who have "stuck it" should be those marked out for hardships and punishment, while those who "chucked up the sponge" are now safely at home.

Lord preserve us! We shall get through it some day.

And that's that—as the coster said when the apples ran down the sewer.

Ribbons

Needless to say, no recommendations have been forwarded. The brigade being judged to have behaved badly, none will be considered. This is a charity to me; but my logic breaks down before the reasoning which concludes that, because a brigade has been foolishly handled or officers have been negligent, no corporal can have done more than his duty.

Ribbons! Could anything be added to make one more cynical about them? If anything were wanted I have only to recollect how those Australians told me (with what truth I do not know) that when a battalion had done well in the line so many decorations were "dished out," and they decided who should have them by the toss of a coin. I shall never see a man wearing the D.C.M. again without thinking of Jackson and successful brigades, or an M.C. without remembering why Rowley sent my name up.

When I told Jackson this morning I had put his name up, but no recommendations were to be forwarded, he looked bored and unconcerned; rather as if I had betrayed his confidence to fools. I had.

The surprise of the day is that Rowley's leave has gone through, and he starts for England to-morrow. He vows he is not coming back, and I do not expect he will. Poor old Rowley! The war has taken full toll of him. A friendly, generous-natured creature, with the Englishman's finest birthright—a sense of fair play—he can afford a few vices, having that superb quality, and right from the beginning, in spite of everything, there has been friendship between us. If only all the affection of which he was capable had been polarised. . . .

Another surprise is that I am to take over the company. Hardy has always acted as second-in-command, but I hear it is the colonel's wish that I should take over. Rowley says the colonel is very pleased with Hardy and me and only wishes he had more like us. I hate to feel ungenerous, but if we are any good, either we have been hiding our wonderful lights under a bushel, or it has taken the colonel a long while to discover them. In spite of this kindness I am not sorry he is leaving the battalion, and but for the fact that I think Hardy's idea of discipline stupidly mechanical, I would as soon he had the company. It will be a thankless and merely temporary appointment. But the men need more consideration than I shall be able to give them, and for this reason I shall be glad to be in charge. Hardy is a sportsman, and I haven't a doubt that we shall work together perfectly amicably.

The pitiable Company

The whole of the company is billeted in one large house. It is a wretched dilapidated place, full of small rooms. The men are packed in it like sardines. Their clothes and equipment are not yet free from the mud of the trenches, which is unbelievably difficult to remove. A number of them really ought to be in hospital. What they want is a few days' complete rest and change. What they are getting is intensive training. The wind of adversity blows hard.

"All officers will attend all parades."

The first parade this morning was at 7.30, and, with the barest intervals for meals, we have been on parade till 7 p.m. Rowley has gone, and Hardy and I curse our luck till we grin. The colonel remains, and this afternoon, *"All officers to the C.O. at 4"* was the preliminary to what will perhaps be his last fulmination. Hardy and I happened to know that we were really exempted from his displeasure, but that made the hearing of it only a little less unpleasant. I do not like his tone. I do not believe the average soldier is the most ungrateful creature in the world. The men are "fed up," and small wonder. Who wouldn't be, on finding himself, after those unspeakable trenches, condemned to ceaseless parades, shut up in this village with no time or scope for any kind of decent recreation or enjoyment? What wonder that they grumble and fill their letters with hopes of leave? It's not discipline, it's change these men need.

If ever I have a company of my own, I know of some essentials to that contentment which is the foundation of all good discipline. A battalion on rest wants a company canteen, a reading- and writing-room with games, inter-platoon and inter-company football matches every free Saturday, musical instruments, a gramophone—anything; and company concerts at least once a week.

Once we get past these eternal inspections—once we get clean and sound again—once we get rid of this colonel, who seems to have a "scunner" on the men, we'll see. To-morrow evening, at any rate, Hardy and I take the company to a divisional entertainment at Molliens Vidames. It is significant that we do so at our own expense.

Court-martial

The battalion is desperately short of officers. It appears that sick officers are kept on the establishment for some time after they have left the regiment, and that there is no such thing as temporary supplies while they are away. At the same time, with idiotic recurrence, orders keep coming to the adjutant to supply officers for the different courses in progress, and though he tears his hair he must find somebody to send. Hardy is the latest requirement. He goes for a Lewis-gun course in a day or two, and that will leave me with the company to myself. In for a penny—in for a pound. What with parades all day and chits from the orderly-room arriving all night, we nearly work the clock round as it is, and we cannot do more. That silver lining hymned in the music-halls at home is about due.

To-day I have had a new experience. Only

this morning I discovered that one of the men of
Hill's platoon was due for a court-martial at Molliens Vidames to-day. Rowley had offered to speak
for the man, and had taken the particulars, but
going suddenly on leave, I suppose he had for-
gotten to hand them on.

I was horrified to find the man was to be on
trial for his life, and actually at 8.45 a.m. of the
same day nothing had been done to prepare his
defence. Moreover things looked very black. He
had slipped away when the battalion was leaving
Caours, taken off his shoulder-straps and escaped
to Paris, where he was arrested ten days later;
and that, after having been "crimed" for absence
without leave twice previously, made a bad case.

I heard what he had to say: handed the company over to Hardy, and trudged the couple of
miles in the rain to Molliens Vidames.

We assembled in the town-hall, which has been
temporarily converted into a music-hall for the
divisional entertainers. The pierrot drapery still
adorned the stage where the court sat. In the
middle of the stage were the judges, consisting
of three senior officers. On the right was our assistant adjutant, prosecuting. In the centre the
prisoner between an armed escort, and on the left
myself in the capacity of "prisoner's friend." A
sergeant of the police as doorkeeper made up
the entire assembly. In such surroundings it

seemed impossible to believe that this man's life hung in the balance.

The evidence was not disputed, and there were no witnesses for the defence. I put the man on oath and gave him leading questions. I wanted to show that, despite appearances, the man had not deserted, but, after getting drunk, had wandered off like a fool, and then, putting off the day when he would have to face the music, had not troubled to seek out the battalion.

According to his own story he had been a miner in civil life. In this occupation he had always earned plenty of money, and drunken bouts between spells of work had become a habit with him which he could not break. When he had finished his confessions I gave evidence on his behalf, saying I knew he was a brave man who had often volunteered for patrols in the trenches.

The prisoner was marched off. I saluted the presiding officer and made my way back here while the court deliberated. I wonder what the result will be? I do hope he will get off, for the man is sound enough when he is sober; but I fancy the decision will turn on whether he actually missed duty in the trenches or not.

The stark crude simplicity of the whole proceedings continues to amaze me. It helps to bring home the fact that life is cheap to-day.

The lost pal

I have the melancholy task of writing to the near relatives of the four men in my platoon who were killed. There is no doubt now that Connor, the only Irishman I had, was killed by one of those whiz-bangs that dropped among us while we were standing outside headquarters. One of the three stretcher-bearers, who was only slightly wounded, has returned. He is certain that the shell which badly wounded Spencer killed Connor. I wonder whether it is any comfort to his wife to know that he was killed after working heroically for three days at a job voluntarily undertaken? I miss Connor. He was characteristic of the most lovable race in the world. Every day now his pal Matthison asks me if I've any news of Connor, and when I say no, he shakes his head and adds, "No, sir, I'm sure he's killed. I said so when he didn't come in."

But every day he repeats the question.

DECEMBER

DECEMBER

"A horse, of course"

I AM COMING TO THE CONCLUSION
that the only man in the British army who
is paid "piecework" is the Deviser of Courses
in this brigade. I, who have never learnt riding,
am just detailed to accompany the transport-
officer to Molliens Vidames for a lecture by the
A.D.V.S. on "The Care of Horses and Stable
Management." Truly one's education is never
complete. The care of men must make shift. Enter
horses.

There are two: the transport-officer's and that
unfortunate beast of the doctor's which recently
came within an ace of drowning in the mud. It
now looks a bag of bones; but Oliver misinterprets
my reluctance to mount by assuring me it is getting
better and the exercise will do it good. I explain
that I have not been in a saddle since the days
when my nurse and the pony-boy led an equally
unfortunate-looking animal between two break-
waters on the sands at Worthing. But Oliver is
very encouraging and we both hope for the best.

Sickness and confinement seem to have given
the doctor's nag an undue affection for his com-

panion's tail. He seems determined to reach it, though I draw the reins to my chest and speak to him ever so kindly. I really must persuade him to walk, for neither he nor I can stand this bumping. Merciful Heavens! I shall break the end of my spine. Bump, bump, bump! I swear, I sweat, I shove my knees together till I wonder they don't meet; I ride with a tight rein and then with a slack one; I rise to it, I fall to it, I lean back, I lean forward; I press in the stirrups, I pretend I have none. It is no good. Do what I may, the ears of this dejected bag of bones prick back towards me like railway-signals and his eye becomes a red lamp.

Leaning along his neck, I suggest to Oliver that perhaps we needn't hurry, and Oliver, being a kindly disposed person, walks his magnetic horse, with most comforting results—for about a dozen yards. But good riders do not, I believe, like walking their horses permanently; so Oliver discovers it is getting late and suggests we might push on. Sticking on is my concern, and whether I shall succeed in this feat grows more and more doubtful as a trot breaks into a canter. Shades of John Gilpin! I wish this beast would keep his eyes and ears to the front. And what are we doing now? Galloping, I do believe. Heavens preserve us!

They do. I do not break my neck. I do not even fall off; but full of gratefulness to God and the

horse, enter the cobbled streets of the town looking as if I had been boiled in oil.

With as much swagger as possible I dismount
and we attend the lecture. What the gentleman
is saying I really cannot now consider, for I live
in fearful anticipation of things to come. I have
just about cooled down when the lecture is over.

Oliver must have heard my prayer during the
lecture, for as we come out he asks me whether
we shall ride back together or whether I would
rather come along on my own. With the air of
one preferring a saddle in the Grand National
to one in the Derby, I reply that I think perhaps
I might as well come along on my own.

Fair and softly now! We shall arrive all in
good time. There is no bewitching tail for you to
follow, and if we are patient with one another, my
poor, dear, kind, terrible bag of bones, we may
come to some understanding of each other's limitations before we reach the nose-bag. Look! we
are gaining confidence already; and now, as you
lightly foot it forward, I declare I should not fear
if home were another half-mile out of sight. However, here we are. Let us be content. I am sure
we both give thanks at having come to the end
of this perilous journey with our lives.

But oh! I wonder, as I get to the ground, what
will happen to my legs on parade to-morrow?
They are stiff as boards, and semicircular.

The new Brigadier

The old brigadier has gone. I have met him two or three times lately, and my hope is that he may live long in the circle of his family, riding to hounds and engaging in those other pursuits for whose performance he was richly endowed by Nature. And may the legend of "the old army" die happy.

Such a fussation last night! Battalion to be inspected by new brigadier to-day. Every scrap of leather to be taken to bits, every speck of mud removed, every man to be rigged out somehow, gas-bags to be worn just so, every round of ammunition to be taken out and cleaned ready for two parades (one at 7.30 and another at 9) to make sure we are all correct.

Then off to the parade-ground this morning, and, once arrived, breathing hardly allowed to spoil our immobility. General salute, march past, and off we go, having learnt from the general that our motto henceforth will be "Keep Smiling." A little trite, perhaps, but highly seasonable, seeing that we haven't been smiled upon for a goodish time.

Is the victim-hunt coming to an end? Devoutly we hope so; for when the heavens are full of thunder and the gods quarrel the lives of men are precarious.

I hear my "deserter" is not to be shot. He is sentenced to two years' hard labour. No one believes he will do it. "Meritorious conduct" in the trenches might wipe out the whole sentence.

Away to Daours

Another triumph on the part of the Deviser of Courses! A junior subaltern is wanted for a general course at Daours, seven miles east of Amiens. Mallow, the late bombing officer, is at a loose end, there being three other officers to his company; so my company is handed over to him (he being a full lieutenant), and I am detailed for the course. The adjutant explains that he is very satisfied with my work, but simply has no one else available and a place must be found for Mallow. What does it matter that I passed through a senior-officer's course in England nine months ago? This will be a change for me.

I begin to feel like Cæsar's dust, except that whereas that immortal clay could stop but one bung-hole, I can fit any. I am very sorry to be relinquishing the company to Mallow, because, although of course he knows the work, and is efficient enough, I dislike the thought of my men being under him.

Apart from that, I am only sorry to be going because it puts leave this year out of sight, and I am fast coming to that stage when the thought of leave becomes an obsession. I still hope to "do my bit in the Great War," and am fully conscious it won't have been done till certain yards of French territory have been regained by efforts wherein I am concerned; but these last few weeks have taken bellyfuls of wind out of my sails. So it seems. Perhaps I should feel differently if I could only get well again.

The colonel goes to-night. Who can be sorry?

I have great satisfaction in the thought that one of my last actions as company-commander is to comply with a request for a "smart N.C.O." for a month's course at Divisional School by sending Jackson. At least he will have a decent billet, good rations and interesting training for a while, and probably receive another stripe when he returns.

I seem to have developed a perfectly fiendish passion for justice. I wonder why?

On dignity of living

In this railway-carriage on the way to Amiens there are a number of French civilians, middle-class people, probably on their way to business. They please me intensely, especially the women.

The woman in the corner might be anything— a typist, an aristocrat, a mother; perhaps she is all three. It has taken generations of culture to produce the dignity of living, the pride of personality and the perfect *savoir faire* she shows. She is beautifully but inexpensively dressed in black, her features are small and refined, and her voice has musical variety, betokening vivacity that is thoroughly enjoyed and at the same time under control. Though I hardly understand a word of her conversation, I should be delighted to listen to her and watch her dignified movements for the rest of the day. Dignity: that is the quality possessed by nearly all these people, and above all others I esteem it. It can only come to those who know the art of living and who, in learning that art, have suffered deeply. Now I reflect that only those who have the sensitiveness common to these people are capable of deep suffering. The boorishness of army life makes one susceptible to this charm, and I am pleased to think that a refined Frenchwoman is possessed of sufficient telepathy to be conscious of my admiration and of sufficient pride to enjoy it.

Treasure in a sack

The school is at a large house standing in its own grounds, about ten minutes' walk from Daours station. The rooms are now bare and rather dilapidated, but the wallpaper and the mirrors suffice to show there has been good living here. I share a small bedroom with three other subalterns. There is not room to swing a cat; but then "room" is a comparative term, as we learn out here, and the rough canvas beds are quite adequate.

Castlereagh having fallen sick, I have been obliged to find another servant. This one, Cox, is a man of forty-three: he has a large family in

England, so I thought practice might have enabled
him to help me take care of myself. And his heart
is good, if his head is never on very active service.

Now, in this small bedroom, he kneels unpack-
ing my valise. Not all my tackle is in it. The tendency of letters and rubbish to accumulate has
crowded three pairs of boots into that sack, which
I gave into his keeping when he got into the train
at Amiens. I can't quite understand it, because the
sack felt very light when I carried it upstairs just
now. However, Cox assures me it's all right. He
cuts the string and fishes for the boots. Slowly his
hand emerges, producing—a large Spanish onion!

We shout with laughter; but though this is a
rich joke, it is also a serious matter, as any soldier
with three pairs of broken-in marching-boots to his
name well knows. Cox goes hareing off to the
railway-station, but I am afraid he will not secure
the boots. I remember a Breton peasant sat opposite him in the carriage, and unless that peasant
has very large feet, or is super-honest, I think he
will appreciate the exchange. His uncooked onions
are not much good to me. Not a subaltern, not
even an orderly, will buy them. I can't even change
them for a gross of green spectacles.

Jerks and drinks

There are about five-and-twenty officers at this
school, and a similar number of N.C.O.s. The
course lasts three weeks. I haven't the energy to

pump up enthusiasm over the work, but we are
a merry band and, perhaps because we are free
from regimental responsibilities, there is more
good humour about than is common, at any rate
to my battalion. Without a wholesome tendency
to rag on any pretext, we should be having a
deadly-dull time since there is nothing essentially
entertaining about getting up before it is light,
having a scrambled breakfast and doing physical
jerks on the frozen lawn outside, especially if you
feel rheumaticky. Similarly, drill, 9–10: bayonet-
fighting, 10.15–11.15: lecture on pay and mess
book, 11.30–12.30: and a similar air with varia-
tions from 2 till 6.30, really isn't exciting when you
have many times repeated these stages of instruction since you entered upon them two years ago.
But here, for the first time in France, I am meeting men on whom a literary allusion is not lost,
and men who can take a rise out of a sergeant-
instructor without impairing his authority or
spoiling good feeling.

In the evenings we are woefully at a loss for
amusement, being restricted to a piano in the
common-room and a French billiard-table in the
small room adjoining. Almost the only practicable
method of showing sociability is to order drinks
and get up to some variety of horseplay. We do
both increasingly as we get to know one another
and the common stock of good will grows, so that
our evenings tend rather in the direction of

drunken carousals. When throats become hoarse
with roaring out songs, and a man of "Pongo's"
elephantine weight begins dancing, we are lucky if
we get to bed before a couple of chairs are broken
and anybody needs assistance up the winding stairs.

The Staff-Captain's lecture

At the Town-hall we attend a lecture by a
divisional staff-captain in a room which is used in
the daytime as a school. The staff-captain is a tall
fair man of aristocratic bearing, keen eyes and a
genial manner. He is talking about the necessity
for keeping the initiative, and pointing out the
many ways in which troops holding the line may
show themselves masters of the situation, even
though the time for an advance over the German
lines be delayed till the Spring. Our one object
should be to prevent the enemy from ever feeling
comfortable, and to this end we should keep
patrols going and raid the enemy trenches whenever there is a chance. *Morale* is the great factor,
and by keeping the initiative we shall help to de-
stroy the German *morale* and so make the work
of advance ten times easier than it would be if,
through slackness, we allowed the other side to
feel themselves "top-dog."

He is tremendously keen, not in the least
ominiscient, and adding to his keenness humour,
and being himself obviously fearless, his words
catch on. One sees the force of his argument, and

the incitement to hold the advantage only seems like the encouragement of a good trainer who wants rugger forwards to use all their weight in the scrum and is able to show them how to do it.

It is not until the lecture is over that one reflects on his advice in terms of actuality. Then one sees a raid as a foul, mean, bloody, murderous orgy which no human being who retains a grain of moral sense can take part in without the atrophy of every human instinct.

I've a desire to go back and tell this gallant gentleman that unless he can infuse into my blood hatred such as I seem psychologically incapable of feeling towards an unknown enemy, much as I should like to be able to help keep the initiative, and quite ready as I am to sacrifice my life for this end, I honestly don't see how it's to be done.

A man of quality

I have been getting to know one of the fellows who shares my room, and now I realise that it is his society that is making this course the pleasantest event I have experienced out here. Superficially he is a very odd mixture. He has been a divinity student, but before the war he had discarded the idea of going into the Church. The experience has left him with a deep reflective streak which lies under the most turbulent high spirits. Dales is the centre of every rag, and he rags with wild zest and absolutely imperturbable good temper; yet ten minutes after pitching himself against impossible odds and being utterly scragged and flattened out, he will lie on his bed ready to talk about classical and modern poetry or the relationship of politics to religion.

He has a laugh. It is uproariously loud, sometimes almost hysterical; but if it were only for his laugh I should choose his company. When he is not amused, his long face is the most serious at the table, and he slips from solemnity to his uproarious mirth at a step. Beer he espouses, quoting Calverley and Belloc in support of his taste, and he assures me there is a mixer of cocktails in Amiens who almost makes the war worth while.

Underneath this boisterous exterior there is one of the gentlest souls I have ever met. He has real feeling for poetry, and the other day confessed to the constant attempt to write it. He will show me nothing of his own, but the other night he wrote out this, which he says he read in the *Saturday Westminster Gazette:*

> *I was a sailor sailing on sweet seas,*
> *Trading in singing birds and humming bees,*
> *But now I sail no more before the breeze.*
>
> *You were a pirate, met me on the sea;*
> *You came with power behind you, suddenly:*
> *You stepped on to my ship and spoke to me,*
> *And while you took my hand and kissed my lips*
> *You sank my ships! You sank my sailing ships!*

He wrote from memory and I copy what he wrote. I believe the little poem epitomises his feeling about the war.

"Leaping upon the spears" is one of his favourite phrases, and he quotes it in connection with the advice about "maintaining the initiative." Certainly I would prefer that exercise in his company to it in any other out here. The man has innate nobility. I learnt slowly how he came to be at the school; for that he should be is surprising, as he has already seen several months' active service in the trenches as a subaltern.

He was wounded in the foot early on July 1st, and, going home, enjoyed himself in hospital and on leave as only Dales could. But some vile pang of conscience made him feel he was too happy for the times; so although he was marked for "home service" he told the doctor he felt fit enough to come out again. His wound has not yet healed and occasionally troubles him, but he makes very light of it. The adjutant of his regiment sent him on to the school really to give the wound a chance to heal.

The canker of war

Dales and I, together with two or three others, have come into Amiens for the week-end, as is the cheering custom of the school. Any vehicle out here serves to give a man a lift, and we all boarded an empty French ambulance which

brought us in. We have booked our rooms at the
hotel and had a bath, wandered round the town,
lined up in a long queue for a hair-cut, and now
sit in a large well-lit restaurant having dinner.

There must be a hundred and fifty officers dining here, fellows from every imaginable regiment,
and we are all doing ourselves very well. Oysters,
salmon mayonnaise, chicken, wine, and again wine
and liqueurs; we neither stint ourselves nor are
stinted. And of all people in the world just now
I suppose we are best able to enjoy a good dinner.
It will cost forty francs, but money has lost its
value, and what man with a good appetite would
not have an expensive dinner if he knew it might
be his last? Let us eat, drink and be merry, for in
a few days we go up the line.

The imminence of fate begets a happy-go-lucky
attitude to life that must breed strange conse-
quences if ever the war is over. The lives of this
company are cheap; and men must wrest some
compensation from the prospect of short life. No
doubt most of these young fellows have come
from sober, English, middle-class homes, but war
has come to give them one crowded hour of in-
glorious life and then an age without a name.

The most feverish among us appear to be in
the Royal Flying Corps. Members of the "Suicide
Club" have more opportunities for this kind of
thing than most of us, and they seem to be making

the best of it. The American Bar was full of them, and here they are, dining as lavishly as the rest of us, though after a day over the enemy lines to-morrow they will again be free to repeat the gaiety, if they are not killed.

The war has cheapened life till it is of little or no value. Life, no doubt, is sweet to all, but no one will persuade me half of these fellows have any real sense of its value. It has become a mere plaything, "merry and bright" while you can keep it, a burst squib if you can't. There is no need to sentimentalise over it and fancy yours is of more value than that of the last man who lost his. Fate plays pitch-and-toss with us: the lighter the coin the more it rings. There's nothing serious left, and if there were, what has it to do with us, except in so far as we retain the regard of men and women as being "the thing"? If this war *is* a drama, well, let it be musical comedy. "Up we go and the best of luck."

Religion, philosophy, the arts: what have they to do with us? Words, words. Are you a good sportsman? That is our test; and a good sportsman rates his life at the value of thistledown, and the lives of the enemy at the price of rats' tails. Cheerio! Let's have another drink. Moreover there are women in Amiens.

So it all appears.

Angle of vision

We are nearing the end of this course. To-day
the corps-commander came and gave us a lecture
on Self-help. He is a man of great reputation,
having won fame at Ypres in 1914, and we were
duly impressed to see him in the flesh walking
and talking like any ordinary mortal. There were
no signs of amazing intellect, but all the characteristics of a well-bred English gentleman—
self-confidence, friendliness, honesty and power of
resistance.

He made no attempt to disguise his obvious
enjoyment of the war, and, for my part, I should
have despised him if he had. It stands to reason
that anyone in his position, so long as he is not
overwhelmed by his responsibility, must be having
the time of his life. For the higher command the
war is the great adventure. Into it they can and
do put tremendous zeal and endless thought. At
the same time they have all the excitement of a
bigger game than any other. They are working
a great business, fascinating to manage, with
prizes of enormous kudos for success. Defeat
would be the certain portion of armies com-
manded by men who did not enjoy their job.

Our lecturer was full of sympathy with the
man in the trenches and of appreciation for his
miseries. He was dead keen that not a single
Tommy should have a worse time than is unavoid-
able, and suggested a variety of useful ways in
which we could mitigate the evils of our lot. But

alas, when he came to our greatest evil—mud—
he made a real *faux pas,* which shows how distance lends enchantment. To get rid of the mud
he suggested we should use biscuit-tins. I am sorry
I could not get up and move as an amendment
that we should use toothpicks. They would be as
serviceable.

The Christmas party

It is Christmas Day. We have spent the morning in bed and the afternoon in slippered idleness
round the fire. Now we are gathered round the
festive board. Other than wine we have no guests;
so we make the best of wine: the toasts are many
and the whiskies double. Rider, a dark-eyed,
genial soul, sits on my right, and the fiery red-
haired Dales on my left. There's a fierce pang as
we drink to Absent Friends, but even that gives
way to merriment. 'Tis mine to propose the commandant's health, and who'd have believed I could
have found so easily-wagging a tongue? There
are many bottles on the table. I arrange them in
a row to illustrate how a great tactician like our
host will use his men. The moves are met with
cheers, and with a fluency I have never found
before, the speech goes on. I see their laughing
faces . . .

Peer through the smoke, the laughter and the wine,
   Twelve months beyond, and where are these that met
In cordial friendship, singing *Auld Lang Syne,*
   Pledging each other never to forget?

Ghosts! Ghosts! they flit about the vacant rooms
  Where Memory wanders, like an ancient crone,
Telling the beads of many different dooms
  In dreary wastes within Death's hungry zone.
The best are dead; and we, who were the rest,
Walk a strange world that is without the best.

New Year's Eve at Corbie

It is New Year's Eve, and we are at Corbie, on the way back to our battalions. Dales and I stroll out to the church of this low-lying town that stands at the meeting of the Somme and the Ancre. In the moonlight we see the big square tower, rising above flat, marshy ground, and it brings to mind the associations of peace and stability, of solid life and spiritual aspiration. Looking in, we see they are preparing for a midnight service. How gladly we would wait and spend the night in here! But not this year. We have appointments with Fate to keep and must be some miles nearer the place of his choice before the bells begin to ring. We hurry back to catch the train.

Rail-head has been moved forward since last I was in these parts, and shortly before midnight the wheezy engine drags us noisily up the hill to Carnoy. The flashes in the sky and the everlasting boom of guns tell us the war is also seeing another New Year in. Of how many more will it take toll?

We call at a signaller's cabin to ask which huts our regiments occupy, and there, with strangers, drink to the coming year while the clock strikes twelve. Another minute and we have all dispersed in the darkness and mud.

JANUARY · 1917

The new broom

$\mathcal{T}$HE BATTALION HAS JUST COME out of the trenches where they have been for two days. Times have changed since our débâcle at Lesbœufs in November. Two days in, two days out, back for two days and then out for a week, is now the order of the times—times which have begotten not only short spells in the trenches, but the most rigorous care and preparation before going up to prevent trench-feet, including the general issue of rubber boots which are given to the men at Ginchy and returned there when they come out of the line.

Not only the times have altered. The battalion seems hardly recognisable with its new colonel, new officers and fresh drafts. Hardy is full of the spirit of the new broom, and all that was gets contrasted very disparagingly with all that now is. Hardy was never anywhere near the front line at Lesbœufs, so perhaps he has some excuse for minimising the iniquities of that place and speaking slightingly of his old captain. But Mallow, who "went sick" after two days of that experience, has less excuse, and betrays himself for

what he is by never losing an opportunity of re-
viling the man who came nearest to being his
sworn companion (at any rate over the bottle)
while he was still here. I do not like men who
only grow great by the infirmities of others. But
I can forgive Hardy because he is young and keen,
and something of the chameleon is natural to
young things.

I see that I have missed the tide by being away
from the regiment when the new colonel arrived.
Whether I belong automatically to the bad old
order or not, I don't know; but in the spring-
cleaning, the old and new furniture found its place
a fortnight ago, and when they celebrated the
occasion I think they omitted the toast of Absent
Friends. No matter. The trenches are fine places
for testing bubble reputations, and I for one am
prepared to accept their judgment.

The colonel appears to be an excellent fellow.
A professional man in civil life, he started in the
army as a subaltern, and now wears the D.S.O.
If his manner is conceited, that is a minor weakness. He is keen and takes an intelligent interest
in the battalion. He has instituted weekly round-
table talks with officers at which the old indis-
criminate cursing is omitted. He has wit and good
humour, and at present is the object of much hero-
worship.

I shall catch the tide when it turns again. Meantime humble-pie has its merits. It is unenvied.

Uncongenial society

Hardy has gone on a month's course to Paris. For the first time I am so companionless I wish myself in any other battalion. Just now the hut contains two of the new officers posted to D Company. They are loud, swaggering, insensitive hulks, very proud of their belts after their apprenticeship as commercial travellers. Preferring the company of gentlefolk, I should be happier living with the men.

I met Dales to-day and went over to his mess. It was a delicious relief. "An officer and a gentleman." It's a matter of character. Without character there can be neither. Men of mean spirit, bearable at other times, become unbearable in the trenches; for in the trenches, want of spirit stinks.

I also ran across "Pongo." He flattered me with the very cream of flattery by begging me to come to dinner at his mess because he wanted me to make an after-dinner speech. I had the greatest difficulty in declining; but success that is due to the length of the bottle might be dismal failure if repeated.

To-night I go up the duck-boards with a fatigue-party carrying barbed wire. Last night I had the whole company out, loading up empty shell-cases on the railway-line over the hill.

Never has the desire for leave been such an obsession. I am almost due for it. Another fortnight and it should come at last.

The Medici prints

My dear in England has sent me half a dozen small Medici prints, and I cannot describe the joy they are to me in this stricken waste. "Beauty is truth—truth, beauty." Here the soul feeds. Here is life's purpose—the creation of beauty. Rubens' babies will never be too fat again: they express the wealth of physical life. Botticelli's women I shall never quarrel with again: they are incarnations of spiritual loveliness. And this girl playing the 'cello to her companion's accompaniment on the harpsichord, what breathing melody the silent picture speaks! Here is the soul of harmony.

Art lives by all that war destroys. Art celebrates or prophesies the perfection of life. War shatters its very fabric and breeds this desolation that now surrounds me to the horizon with a blasting ugliness that has made what is our haven for the moment a hideous corrugated-iron Armstrong hut.

Dignity and impudence

This afternoon we marched to Guillemont, where we are spending the night (those who are not "on fatigue") in shelters that are half dugouts. Shells dropped in Trônes Wood as we came by, but otherwise the march was uneventful.

At dusk on the road outside I saw an incident that gave me a certain malicious pleasure. Major

Smythe was coming along with his orderly. A very
tired-looking Australian, returning from the line,
passed them on the road. He failed to salute. He
was a small, tired man; I doubt if he even saw
more than the boots of our tall major. The major
called to him, but the man merely looked round
and walked on. Whereupon the orderly was sent
with a message. He returned, and the irate major
stood looking furiously after the delinquent, who
turned once more, this time merely to extend his
fingers to his nose after the vulgar manner. There
was not a military policeman in sight, so the incident closed pleasantly. A most ill-disciplined ges-
ture: still, vulgarity has its uses.

Lying in a rough bunk, I've been reading Con-
rad's *Victory*. The coming and going all round,
and the tremor made by a big gun that has its
emplacement very near, made it difficult to get
into the book, but I hung on, determined to see
if an imaginative experience wasn't possible out
here. Although I succeeded, I was disappointed.
It's not a real romance but only a pumped-up
literary effort: effective, strained, and finally, of
course, melodramatic. No doubt it would pass
muster in a drawing-room: here it seems a thin,
"drawn," hot-house plant; the laboured psy-
chology is merely poverty-stricken analytics.

Literary veneer does not change the nature of
the shilling shocker.

In a Flers dug-out

As a battalion we tramped the old duck-boards again yesterday afternoon, and now we've two companies in the front line (this time to the right of Lesbœufs) and one in the second, where there is a big new dug-out. C Company is back in reserve, doing fatigues at night, salving during the daytime and occupying a large dug-out, with officers at one end and men at the other, at a spot near Flers called Bull Dump.

Outside it is snowing gently. There is wrath and recrimination within; for, after carrying a rum-jar right up here, somebody set it down on a stone and the earth has drunk most of the rum. I think the men would forget the tragedy, only the strong odour pervades the place and they are not philosophic enough to be content with smell instead of taste.

Now they have begun to talk about the Kaiser's peace proposals. It is pathetic to hear their comments. I wonder how much of their present desire for peace is due to want of rum.

Dull work

The cold turned to rain, and after two days of duck-board tramping, carrying wire, stakes, rations, bombs and duck-boards up to the front line, we came out in the rain and just had time to get clean and look round the town of hutments that is now Carnoy, before we were ready to go back to the line.

Last night I had to take a party up and now we're going up again. I am tired: physically and mentally tired. Leave deferred maketh the heart sick. I am sick of the energy of those belching guns firing over our heads as we tramp the never-ending duck-boards. I am utterly tired of the mechanical routine of this existence.

We are for the front line. Mallow is in command and I am the only other officer.

Shell-hole trenches

There are no regular trenches here: what we hold is really a rough line of converted shell-holes. Last night I explored the place, stodging through the mud from one post to the next. I ran into the colonel, armed with a pole, ploughing his way along. He was willing to talk of leave and very nice about it, saying I should get my chance all right in a few days.

Mallow has a small dug-out here, which he occupied yesterday evening; but during the night he withdrew the right half-company and himself to the second-line dug-out (we can only move here under cover of dark), for there is to be a bombardment this morning of a German sap that has been advanced towards our line on the right. I am in charge of the left half-company till Mallow comes back to-night.

The end of the journey

Noon. The "show" has begun. Our artillery is making rare good shooting. Boards go up in the air and there's a regular strafe on our right. But the usual retaliation has also begun, and heavy shells are beginning to drop about. We have a tiny corrugated-iron shelter here, made for the signallers. There are two of them and three other men beside myself in the shelter. I think we had better move out of this. Crack! Hullo! What's that? Looking up we see a hole in the iron just over the place where I had been sitting. Something must have come through there. Going back I find a hole in the clay seat on which I had been sitting ten seconds before, and putting my arm a foot into the wet clay draw out the great jagged rim of a shell. It is still warm.

"Get out of this, you fellows, and spread yourselves down the trench.—That's it!—Get some distance between you. Look there, Burt, you've water-boots on. You can go through the water down to . . ."

*   *   *   *   *

What's happened? I am lying on a duck-board looking up at the sky. Dusk is falling. There's a young lance-corporal looking down at me as if I were a curiosity. I ask him what has happened.

"You bin knocked out," he replies smiling. "We thought you was dead."

Something has happened, but I can't remember what. There's been a great nothingness, and I cannot remember what happened before it. I seem to have been dead, and death apparently is nothingness. Why can't that fool stop grinning and tell me just what's happened?

He says I've got the company. I don't know what the devil he means. I never had a company in the line. Oh! I know. This is Hébuterne. 'Fall': 'Fame': 'Fate.'

"Where's Mr. Hill?"

The boy grins.

"Gone back home long since."

"Where's Mr. Smalley?"

He grins again.

"Gone back to Blighty, sir. He went weeks ago."

This is maddening. I tell him to go to blazes and find somebody who can tell me what has happened.

My head is like a furnace: yet it feels as if it were made of jelly, and hullo! my ears are bleeding. Gradually I begin to remember.

I get up and find there are three wounded men here. They say a shell came over and dropped right in the parapet in front of me, wounding those in either side and flattening me out against the back of the trench. There's a great hole just over there, so I suppose that's what happened. The shelter has clean gone.

Darkness begins to come on. The wounded men go back; luckily they can all walk. I am all right now, except that I can't keep awake. What I wonder is, whether the colonel will let me have leave right away, as soon as we come out.

Mallow returns, and I tell him I shall be all right after I have had a sleep. I follow him back to his dug-out, slowly because something's happened to my right leg and I am frightfully stiff. He gives me a drink of cocoa and I fall asleep.

Now he wants me to go back to the dug-out in the second line. Why should I? I only want a good sleep. No, I will sleep. He wakes me again, saying I'd better see the doctor. Reluctantly I try to get out of the dug-out; but it's dark outside and I can't see the way. I come back and, telling him I'll go when the moon gets up, fall asleep again. Again he wakes me and this time I go in company with a runner. Jog, jog, jog. My head aches; but I should have been quite all right. I could have waited till to-morrow.

Here's the second-line dug-out. I crawl down the steps, and some ministering angel gives me another drink. Now I can go to sleep.

No. The colonel passes overhead and sends down word to me to go back to the doctor.

Trudge, trudge, trudge: every step is one less to be taken. And here at last is the old dug-out. The doctor's asleep. Then let him sleep; only give me somewhere to lie down. The M.O.'s orderly comes worrying. The doctor wants to see me now. I pick myself up again. He plasters up my ears and then tells me I had better go to the dressing-station. They will probably put me into hospital to rest for a few days.

Rest? I want no rest in hospital. I want to go home on leave. Damn it! They can't cut out my leave for hospital.

The medical-officer at the dressing-station wants to know what has happened. I tell him all I know and then beg him to let me have just a week's home-leave. He is very sympathetic, but says he can only send me on to the base hospital at Bray.

Now in an ambulance, rattling along. This is comparative comfort. Now a large marquee with beds, and there's a nurse. She tells me to get into that one. God! The comfort and ease! I sleep at last for twenty-four hours straight off.

Rouen

I am in bed at Rouen No. 4 General Hospital feeling rather a fraud, for I've every limb intact and only a dull headache and a thick ear. I slept for two days at Bray. Then I was so stiff they carted me out and brought me here on a stretcher.

There's a colonel of the Gordon's opposite. He is sick. We are a mixed crowd of sick and wounded.

The doctor comes round and I tell him all I know.

"People who lose their memories go home," he replies, as if he were uttering a threat.

Home! My God! I am going home!

le Havre

We are on the ambulance-train travelling to le Havre. A whole week I have been at Rouen eating my heart out for this hour. Now the train crawls on, stopping continually. We shall get there if we've patience.

Yes. This is le Havre. It is nearing midnight. We have just missed a boat. That is the *Glenesk Castle,* and we are now going on board. Down below, everybody! Here are cots, packed tight together so that there is only just room for the nurse to move between them. I can get into my own cot without help, thanks very much. That dark fellow, looking so ill, is a German officer.

I am asleep before the boat moves.

The cliffs

Breakfast in the saloon—a very nice breakfast, beautifully served. We are well on the way. Now up on deck. The sea is like a mill-pond. It is cold and there is no sun. Some officers are playing cards in that little cabin. I watch them like a ghost, and then turn away to come out on deck again.

There, through the grey mists, I see the cliffs. My whole body trembles.

I wonder where the battalion is. It is going to snow. I believe they are going to Sailly-Saillisel. I wonder if Jackson has been made a sergeant.

———————

Made in the USA
San Bernardino, CA
17 September 2014